THINKING ABOUT EDUCATION SERIES
SECOND EDITION
Jonas F. Soltis, *Editor*

The revised and expanded Second Edition of this series builds on the strengths of the First Edition. Written in a clear and concise style, these books speak directly to preservice and in-service teachers. Each offers useful interpretive categories and thought-provoking insights into daily practice in schools. Numerous case studies provide a needed bridge between theory and practice. Basic philosophical perspectives on teaching, learning, curriculum, ethics, and the relation of school to society are made readily accessible to the reader.

PERSPECTIVES ON LEARNING
D. C. Phillips and Jonas F. Soltis

THE ETHICS OF TEACHING
Kenneth A. Strike and Jonas F. Soltis

CURRICULUM AND AIMS
Decker F. Walker and Jonas F. Soltis

SCHOOL AND SOCIETY
Walter Feinberg and Jonas F. Soltis

APPROACHES TO TEACHING
Gary D. Fenstermacher and Jonas F. Soltis

THE ETHICS
═══ OF ═══
TEACHING

SECOND EDITION

KENNETH A. STRIKE
Cornell University

JONAS F. SOLTIS
Teachers College, Columbia University

Teachers College, Columbia University
New York and London

Published by Teachers College Press, 1234 Amsterdam Avenue, New York, N.Y. 10027

Library of Congress Cataloging-in-Publication Data
Strike, Kenneth A.
    The ethics of teaching / Kenneth A. Strike, Jonas F. Soltis. —
2nd. ed.
        p.   cm. — (Thinking about education series)
    Includes bibliographical references (p.   ) and index.
    ISBN 0-8077-3141-2
    1. College teachers—Professional ethics—United States—Case
studies.   I. Soltis, Jonas F.   II. Title.   III. Series.
LB1779.S73   1991
174′.9372—dc20   91-21240

ISBN 0-8077-3141-2

Manufactured in the United States of America

99 98 97 96 95 94 93   2 3 4 5 6 7 8

Contents

Acknowledgments

We would like to thank The Hasting Center Institute of Society, Ethics, and the Life Sciences for bringing us together and starting us thinking about the ethics of teaching at a conference entitled "Professional Ethics in Schools of Education" held in October 1981. We must also thank the many students who attended our classes and helped us to develop and test our approach and materials in Education 472 (Cornell) and TF4680 (Teachers College, Columbia). Some students were kind enough to let us use cases they had constructed: Randy Berger, Tim Counihan, Ann Marie Kelley, Meg Lavigne, Karley Meltzer, Barbara Reynolds, Scott Smith, and Steve Tobolsky. We also had the benefit of seeing some of the cases developed in the Ohio State project on Moral Negotiation. For that we thank Bernard Rosen, Gerald Reagan, and Jo Ann Freiberg. Very special thanks goes to Andrew Alexander, Paul Green, and Tim Counihan, who served as research assistants doing everything including finding sources, copy editing, and offering suggestions. Tim Counihan, who was with the project from start to finish, also ably assisted in ethics courses at Teachers College and skillfully developed and edited cases, some of which appear in this text. Jo Ellen Thomas and Berni Oltz prepared the manuscript, asked some very good questions, and made useful suggestions. Many people read and commented on the manuscript. Among them were Barry Bull, Scott Bilow, Martha Cummings, James Galt, Emil Haller, John Decker, Charles Love, Naomi Mascarenhas, Margaret McCasland, Karley Meltzer, David Monk, George Posner, Vern Rockcastle, Merrill Stevenson, Abebetch Tadesse, Craig Thurtell, and Michael Weinstock.

We also would like to thank Tom Rotell, former Director of the Teachers College Press, and Carole Saltz, the current Director, who supported and encouraged the development of this series, Thinking About Education, as well as Sarah Biondello, Executive Acquisitions

Editor, who encouraged this second edition and involved TC Press in additional books on ethics and education. Finally, we thank Susan Liddicoat of TC Press for her overseeing and caretaking of the second editions of the whole series.

Code of Ethics of the Education Profession

Adopted by the 1975 NEA Representative Assembly

PREAMBLE

The educator, believing in the worth and dignity of each human being, recognizes the supreme importance of the pursuit of truth, devotion to excellence, and the nurture of democratic principles. Essential to these goals is the protection of freedom to learn and to teach and the guarantee of equal educational opportunity for all. The educator accepts the responsibility to adhere to the highest ethical standards.

The educator recognizes the magnitude of the responsibility inherent in the teaching process. The desire for the respect and confidence of one's colleagues, of students, of parents, and of the members of the community provides the incentive to attain and maintain the highest possible degree of ethical conduct. The Code of Ethics of the Education Profession indicates the aspiration of all educators and provides standards by which to judge conduct.

The remedies specified by the NEA and/or its affiliates for the violation of any provision of this Code shall be exclusive and no such provision shall be enforceable in any form other than one specifically designated by the NEA or its affiliates.

Reprinted from *NEA Handbook, 1977–78*, Washington, DC: National Education Association. Used by permission.

PRINCIPLE 1

Commitment to the Student

The educator strives to help each student realize his or her potential as a worthy and effective member of society. The educator therefore works to stimulate the spirit of inquiry, the acquisition of knowledge and understanding, and the thoughtful formulation of worthy goals.

In fulfillment of the obligation to the student, the educator—

1. Shall not unreasonably restrain the student from independent action in the pursuit of learning.
2. Shall not unreasonably deny the student access to varying points of view.
3. Shall not deliberately suppress or distort subject matter relevant to the student's progress.
4. Shall make reasonable effort to protect the student from conditions harmful to learning or to health and safety.
5. Shall not intentionally expose the student to embarrassment or disparagement.
6. Shall not on the basis of race, color, creed, sex, national origin, marital status, political or religious beliefs, family, social or cultural background, or sexual orientation, unfairly:
   a. Exclude any student from participation in any program;
   b. Deny benefits to any student;
   c. Grant any advantage to any student.
7. Shall not use professional relationships with students for private advantage.
8. Shall not disclose information about students obtained in the course of professional service, unless disclosure serves a compelling professional purpose or is required by law.

PRINCIPLE II

Commitment to the Profession

The education profession is vested by the public with a trust and responsibility requiring the highest ideals of professional service.

In the belief that the quality of the services of the education profession directly influences the nation and its citizens, the educator shall exert every effort to raise professional standards, to promote a climate that encourages the exercise of professional judgment, to achieve conditions which attract persons worthy of the trust to careers in education, and to assist in preventing the practice of the profession by unqualified persons.

In fulfillment of the obligations to the profession, the educator—

1. Shall not in an application for a professional position deliberately make a false statement or fail to disclose a material fact related to competency and qualifications.
2. Shall not misrepresent his/her professional qualifications.
3. Shall not assist entry into the profession of a person known to be unqualified in respect to character, education, or other relevant attribute.
4. Shall not knowingly make a false statement concerning the qualifications of a candidate for a professional position.
5. Shall not assist a noneducator in the unauthorized practice of teaching.
6. Shall not disclose information about colleagues obtained in the course of professional service unless disclosure serves a compelling professional purpose or is required by law.
7. Shall not knowingly make false or malicious statements about a colleague.
8. Shall not disclose information about students obtained in the course of professional service, unless disclosure serves a compelling professional purpose or is required by law.

Chapter 1

What This Book Is About

This is a book about the ethics of teaching. You already may know that there is a code of ethics for educators. In fact, the National Education Association Code appears at the beginning of this book. But we are less concerned with your learning the code than in getting you to think about ethics and educating on your own. Ethical thinking and decision making are not just following the rules.

To get you in the right frame of mind and to see what this book is about, let us start with an imaginary situation that could have occurred just as easily on your campus as in our imaginations. As you read it, try to put yourself in the place of the young beginning instructor and ask yourself what would you have done if you were she.

Cynthia Allen was a new instructor in the English department and not much older than her students. She took on the task of teaching the required introductory literature and composition courses with zest and with hours and hours of careful class preparation. However, like many beginning teachers, she soon learned that enthusiasm, hard work, and planning are not always guarantees of success. Some students were bright and performed very well in class. She thought they probably would do just as well no matter who taught the course. Other students, however, did not seem to learn what she tried so hard to teach them. Their work was average or below average, and they sat in the classroom with little to say. She did not know if these students were lost or bored or did not understand her, but she knew that any improvement in this group would please her very much and mark her success as a beginning instructor—if she could only reach them.

The course requirements were four short essays and a final term paper. Cynthia thought this would be a fair evaluation system because it allowed for improvement if a student had not done well at first. The final papers were due on the last day of class, and all the students dutifully handed them in. Having said good-bye to her home-for-the-holidays-bound students, Cynthia turned to the task of reading the final papers and calculating course grades, which were due in the registrar's office within 48 hours.

Reading the first paper, she received a great surprise: Henry, an important new member of the college basketball team, had shown remarkable improvement in his work. Cynthia had found him to be an earnest student during the term, but his schedule of practice and travel made it difficult for him to keep up with classwork. His earlier grades had been *D*, *D+*, *C−*, and *C*. She knew it was necessary for Henry to maintain a *C* average in order to remain eligible for intercollegiate sports and to retain his scholarship. She read his final paper with great concern and hope that soon turned to joy and surprise. It clearly was an *A* paper!

In fact, it was so good that in order to comment on it intelligently, Cynthia had to consult a standard reference book on the topic. There, again to her surprise, she discovered Henry had copied much of his paper directly from the text. It was a clear case of plagiarism.

In addition to a sense of hurt, anger, and failure, Cynthia realized she now had an obligation to the institution. The policy on academic dishonesty was clear:

> The penalty for a proven case of academic dishonesty is an *F* in the course. No provision can be made for a student's withdrawal. The faculty member alleging dishonesty will notify, in writing, the student, the dean of students, and the faculty member's department chairperson. Such notification will become part of the dean's official file on the student, but will not be transmitted outside the university.

The policy on cheating was clear, but Cynthia had some doubts. She was not sure such harsh measures were appropriate in this case or would accomplish desirable educational goals. Following normal procedures would seem to result in a very drastic penalty. If reported and proven to be cheating, Henry would lose his scholarship and probably have to leave school; and the basketball team would lose a valuable player just at tournament time. For other students, one *F* might not be such a burden. For Henry it would be a disaster. What would you do if you were Cynthia?

Stop for a moment and think about this predicament. If you can, discuss it with your roommate or a classmate. If you could take some time to think and talk about it, it would soon become clear that a number of ethical principles and values are at issue here: honesty and dishonesty on the part of both the student and the instructor; obligations to an institution whose rules one presumably agrees to follow by becoming a member, either as a student or as a faculty member; concern for a student's well-being and the recognition of students as persons with lives outside the classroom and with futures that teachers can influence beyond measure.

There are a number of issues and options to unravel. The NEA code does not seem to be of much help, lacking an explicit rule to cover this situation. Implicitly it seems to take the position that teachers should act toward students with the welfare of the student as their primary concern. It also generally requires that teachers act honestly and with integrity in professional matters. Ordinarily we would all agree that honesty and the student's welfare are important values. But when they clash, as they do in this case, then consulting a code or agreeing on values will not help in deciding what to do as much as will some hard ethical thinking—and that is what this book will help you understand how to do.

If Cynthia does not fail Henry and report him because she feels the punishment is too great in this case, she would be paying more attention in her thinking to the harmful consequences of her actions than to the obligation she has to obey the rules. In this book we will call such ethical thinking *consequentialist*. If, however, she takes seriously her personal sense of honesty and her professional obligation to maintain and administer the academic code of her institution fairly to all, she would reach her decision as a *nonconsequentialist*, one for whom duty, obligation, and principle are more important considerations than consequences.

By using three case studies like this one, we will explore ethical problems in teaching that center around the ideas of punishment, intellectual freedom, and equality in the treatment of students. When reading them, you will have to use your imagination and project yourself into the role of the teacher. Then you will have to do some hard ethical thinking yourself. You should also try imagining that you are the student in these cases. Sometimes ethical considerations look different from the perspective of a different person in the situation. In the above case, try imagining you are Henry, a talented minority student with a sick mother who sees his only chance to make something of his life in becoming a professional basketball player. For Henry, it is a case of staying in school with a shot at the pros or going back to the ghetto and a life of menial labor or chronic unemployment. How would you support your diabetic widowed mother? You have a $D+/C-$ average going into the final paper. You have to pull a high grade to get your average up to stay in school and play ball. You know that treating a source as if it were your own work is wrong, but you have been improving and honestly passing the course so far. What would you do?

Using case studies will help put you in a thinking mood. In this book we will use them extensively to display ethical theories and ways of ethical thinking and to present cases for you and your classmates to grapple with on your own. The case studies in Chapters 2, 3, and 4 will supply a context for understanding some major ways ethical theorists have thought about the issues of punishment, freedom, and equality.

These chapters will follow a simple pattern designed to inform and challenge your thinking. First, there will be a "Case" that, like the case of Cynthia Allen in this chapter, sets up the ethical dilemma. Next, there will be an imaginary "Dispute" that lays out some of the ethical issues of the case in an intuitive way. Disputes will be similar to the kinds of discussions that occur in a dorm room or in a teachers' lounge when people sense something is morally amiss and argue over what is ethically problematic. This will give you a feeling for what is at issue. Then a discussion of ethical "Concepts" relevant to the dilemma will provide an opportunity for you to see how major ethical theories throw some light on the issues. These theories will deal not only with what is to be considered right or wrong, but also with how we can decide what is right or wrong. Understanding the thinking of major ethical theorists will help you see some options open to you as an ethical thinker. In the next section, called "Analysis," we will show you what it would be like to think about and reach a decision using the consequentialist and the nonconsequentialist perspectives, as well as the principles of respect for persons and benefit maximization. We will also reflect on the nature of ethical thinking itself. Finally, at the end of each chapter and in the last part of the book we will provide additional case studies for class discussions.

But before we begin our treatment of cases, it is important to make you aware that this book also treats another theme that is very crucial to contemporary thinking about professional ethics and ethics in general. Most people probably would agree that teachers should behave in an ethical manner. Many people also might have serious doubts that questions about ethical behavior can be settled objectively. Perhaps you are one of those people. "After all," you might say, "aren't questions of ethics really questions of personal values or the values of the group to which one belongs?" "Is there really an objective right or wrong in human affairs?" "Doesn't it really just come down to what one believes is right or wrong?" "Isn't it wrong for one person to try to impose his or her values on someone else?"

We are aware that subjectivism and relativism are serious contemporary concerns. To the modern ear, the claim that one should do such and such because it is the right thing to do sounds intolerant and dogmatic. Why should someone else's opinion be better than yours? Can we be tolerant without being relativistic? Can we be objective without being certain? These are disturbing, but important, considerations that no serious discussion of ethics today can avoid.

Therefore, we believe that if we are to be successful in getting you to think effectively about professional ethics, we will have to persuade you that questions of ethics can be objectively discussed and morally justified courses of action undertaken. In what follows, we shall try to do just that, but ultimately you must be the judge. We believe that a kind of rational ethical thinking that goes beyond personal beliefs and values is essential both to professional ethics and to the moral education of all members of society. Ethics is a public as well as a personal matter. If we are correct, then it would seem to follow that teachers have a special obligation to help their students see and share the potential objectivity and rationality of ethical thinking so that we can all lead morally responsible lives together. That is also what this book is about.

THE NATURE OF ETHICAL INQUIRY

The Code of Ethics of the National Education Association contains the following statement: "The educator . . . shall not deliberately suppress or distort subject matter relevant to the student's progress." All of us probably believe this. It certainly seems wrong to lie to or deceive students. One might quibble, of course. Is it always wrong? How are we to decide when deliberate distortion has occurred? We suspect, however, that there will be few who will wish to defend the general merits of deceiving students, no matter what their quibbles may be.

We also suspect that agreement can be reached on another claim about this statement. It is an ethical statement. It is not a description of what the world is like. Instead, it tells us what we ought to do.

These observations about this statement from the NEA Code raise two questions. First, what makes this claim an ethical one, and, second, how do we know that it is true? Let us start with the first question.

What makes a claim an ethical claim? To answer that, we need to know what ethics is about. Some obvious things come to mind. Ethics concerns what kinds of actions are right or wrong, what kind of life is a good life, or what kind of person is a good person. All of these things seem clear enough. Our thinking will be advanced, however, if we can distinguish ethical claims from two other sorts of claims.

Ethical claims need first to be distinguished from factual ones. Facts tell us something about the world. They describe. They are true when the world is the way they say it is. Otherwise they are false. The claim "the world is round" is true because the world is round, and the claim "the world is flat" is false because the world is round. Claims about what is right and wrong seem not to describe in this way. They are not true because they correctly describe some part of the world. They do not tell us how the world is, but how it ought to be. Thus they prescribe, not describe. When someone behaves in a way that is different from how people ought to behave, an ethical standard is violated, but that standard does not become false because the world turns out to be different from that which is prescribed. That people sometimes lie or steal does not falsify the duty to be honest.

Because moral claims are not facts does not mean that they cannot be true or false, however. It only means that they cannot be true or false in the same way that facts are. We do not decide if ethical claims are true or false by seeing if they correspond to the world. How we do decide if they are true or false is a story for later.

It is also important to distinguish ethical claims from appraisals or preferences. Perhaps the need to do this is not obvious. Most of us are used to thinking of ethical judgments, appraisals, and preferences as "values." Nevertheless, an example may suggest why it is useful to distinguish ethical claims from these other kinds of "values." Suppose I have a friend who is an excellent skier. One day as I see him flying down the slope, I remark, "My, he's a good skier." Now think how odd it would be to treat this remark as a comment about his character, as though I had said, "My, he's a good person." The word *good* is a general word of appraisal. Sometimes we use it in an ethical way. We do this when we want to approve the rightness of an action or the moral qualities of a person. For example, we are likely to describe individuals who are unusually kind or who devote their lives to helping others as good people. But we can also use *good* to say that someone excels at something even when we find the activity quite reprehensible on moral grounds. "He's a good burglar" tells us that a person is competent at a form of theft, not that we approve of theft or believe that theft is morally acceptable.

There is one type of value judgment from which it is particularly important to distinguish ethical claims. These are judgments about what we like or want (or what we ought to like or want). These judgments concern preferences. Here, too, a few examples should suggest that judgments about preferences are quite different from ethical judgments. It would be absurd, for example, to treat someone's claim to like ice cream as a claim concerning the morality of ice cream. Conversely, it is quite possible to find doing the right thing distasteful or unpleasant.

We believe that we have a moral obligation to pay our income tax. We nevertheless dislike paying it a great deal. We believe that we have a moral obligation to grade our students fairly, that is, to give them what they deserve. We would prefer to give them all *A*'s. Moral judgments are not, therefore, statements of preference or taste.

What kinds of judgments are they? Fundamentally, they are statements of obligation. Moral judgments tell us what we ought to do and what we ought not to do. They tell us what our duties are. We have insisted that ethical claims are not just statements about what kinds of behavior we like, approve of, or judge to be excellent or competent. We believe that the tendency to lump ethical judgments under the general class of value judgments and then to treat all value judgments alike is the source of much confusion about ethics. People tend to assume that value judgments are subjective matters. Indeed, it is often believed that they are rightfully a matter of free choice on our part. It is then assumed to be wrong to impose our values on others. These ideas are not always true.

Such thoughts about subjectivity and free choice are often true of preferences. Surely, it would be absurd to hold that it is right to like olives and wrong to like pickles. There is no right or wrong about it. Moreover, an olive lover who set out to compel another person to share this taste would surely violate that person's rights. On the other hand, it is equally absurd to think that the question of whether or not one should be honest is like the question of whether or not one should like olives. It makes good sense to tell someone who feels no obligation to be honest that honesty is a duty. Moreover, it is often reasonable to enforce honesty against those who would choose to be dishonest.

All of this is to say we must not be seduced by the label *value* into thinking that all value judgments are matters of arbitrary choice and that there is no right or wrong about them. That may or may not turn out to be true. We may fail to show that any moral values can be justified. But we should not uncritically assume that they are unjustifiable at the outset because we confuse moral judgments with preferences.

There are other possibly good reasons to be suspicious about the objectivity of ethical judgments. The Scottish philosopher David Hume (1711–1776) provided one powerful argument.[1] It is sometimes called the "is to ought" fallacy. Hume noted that valid arguments have an interesting property. All of the terms that occur in the conclusion of

---

1. David Hume, *An Inquiry Concerning Human Understanding* (New York: Liberal Arts Press, 1957).

valid arguments are contained in the premises of that argument. We see how this is so in the following standard textbook argument:

All men are mortal.
Socrates is a man.
Therefore, Socrates is mortal.

If the argument were slightly changed, we would see a conclusion that did not follow from the premises in the argument (even though it might be true). Consider:

All men are mortal.
Socrates is mortal.
Therefore, Socrates' dog is mortal.

We cannot reach a valid conclusion about Socrates' dog unless the dog is referred to in the premises of the argument. Valid arguments, after all, tell us what follows from our premises; and things only follow if they are there to begin with. Noting this, Hume then pointed out that it is impossible for any argument containing only factual premises to lead validly to a conclusion about what we ought to do. For any such argument has a new idea in the conclusion that was not in the premises—the idea of obligation. 'Ought' conclusions, according to Hume, cannot follow from 'is' premises.

We need to be clear about what follows from Hume's argument. Hume's argument does not show that ethical knowledge is impossible. What it does show is that ethical knowledge cannot be entirely based on factual knowledge. But what other kind of knowledge is there?

Some philosophers have concluded from this that ethical arguments are possible only if we begin with some initial ethical assumptions. Once we accept some such assumptions, we can use facts to reason to other ethical conclusions. For example, if we begin with the assumption that it is wrong to cause pain, then we can use the factual claim that humiliation causes pain to reason to the conclusion that it is wrong to humiliate people. All ethical arguments, however, begin with an arbitrary and unprovable assumption. If someone, a sadist for example, does not agree with our initial assumption, we have nothing further to say. No argument for the starting point is possible.

This seems very unsatisfactory. Can our ethical conclusions be any better than our premises? Aren't our conclusions just as arbitrary as our initial assumptions? This position seems to lead us to total skepticism. We cannot really know anything in ethics. We can only deliberate with others about what is right and wrong if we already agree with them about our basic assumptions. Perhaps ethical judgments are a matter of personal preference after all.

Before we surrender too quickly to this viewpoint, we should consider what follows from it. Ask yourself if you would be willing to treat some action that you take to be unquestionably evil as a simple difference of taste. We believe that murdering innocent children and putting poison into medicine bottles is wrong. Is that simply an arbitrary assumption on our part, or is it really wrong? Can we know it is wrong? Or are we to conclude that the difference between the Hitlers of the world and decent people is merely that they have different preferences?

If the conclusion of skepticism is hard to swallow, perhaps we should try a different approach. Interestingly, even skeptics and ethical relativists, when they are trying to decide what to do rather than being theoretical and philosophical, seem to be willing and able to consider ethical arguments. How do they do this? In our everyday thinking we and they do not simply treat ethical matters as arbitrary. We all devote a good deal of effort to deciding what is right and what ought to be done. Moreover, we often appear to succeed. Are we simply deluded?

We have a proposal to make at this point. Let us defer the question of whether ethics is possible and look at some real ethical disputes. While we are discussing these issues, we can also look aside from time to time to see how we are actually proceeding. We can try to describe how we are thinking and what the properties of real ethical arguments are. When we have done this, we can return to the question of whether it is possible to think about ethical issues objectively. It is not an issue that can be settled easily. It will take a lot of thinking and considering. But how we settle it will make an important difference in how we think and act in ethical situations as teachers and as human beings.

A CASE

Ms. Jones had not met Johnnie's father. She had spoken on the phone to him several times. In fact, she had spoken to him only half an hour ago. She had told him that Johnnie had been in a fight and that she wished to discuss Johnnie's conduct with him.

Johnnie was often in fights. Not that he was a bad kid. He did not pick on other children or deliberately provoke confrontations. He was just a bit excitable. If he ever suspected that he was being laughed at or criticized, he would charge in swinging. He had not damaged anyone yet. In fact, since he was a small child, he was often the loser. Ms. Jones had once asked him to consider the fact that if he attacked less, he would be beaten up less. Johnnie had only given her a wry smile and said, "I'm used to it." As Johnnie's father charged into her office, that "I'm used to it" took on a whole new meaning. Mr. Pugnacious stood in her doorway with his belt in his hand. All 6'5" of him quivered with wrath as he demanded to have his son turned over to him. "I'll teach that little brat to fight in school," he bellowed. "Where is he?"

Ms. Jones quietly responded that she had not called him so that he would beat Johnnie. She merely wanted to discuss his problem. "What's to discuss?" Mr. Pugnacious answered. "This belt will say it all." The odor beginning to fill the room gave reason to suspect that Mr. Pugnacious was not exactly a model of sobriety.

"But Johnnie didn't start it," Ms. Jones blurted out. "He was beaten up by another boy for no reason. I called you to take him home so that the other boy would not get him after school."

This seemed to suggest a new problem to Mr. Pugnacious. Putting on his belt he asked again to see his son. As he and Ms. Jones walked toward Johnnie's classroom, Mr. Pugnacious began telling Ms. Jones how he planned to teach Johnnie to fight "like a man." Johnnie was to take "no guff off nobody."

Now Ms. Jones began to wonder why she had told Mr. Pugnacious that others had started the fight. She knew that this time the fight had been entirely Johnnie's fault. He had walked into the room obviously upset about something. He had seen several boys in the corner joking. The moment they had broken out laughing, he had charged into the group throwing punches and screaming, "I'll teach you to make fun of me." The boys who were attacked fought back, perhaps too enthusiastically, but they certainly had not started the fight. Ms. Jones found it hard to blame them if they had gotten in a few extra licks.

What really bothered Ms. Jones was that she had lied to Mr. Pugnacious. She considered herself to be an honest person and strongly believed that it was wrong to lie. Indeed, before today, she would very likely have said that lying was always wrong. But she lied to prevent Johnnie from receiving another beating. What good would it have done to tell Mr. Pugnacious the truth? His violent attitudes and actions were probably the source of Johnnie's problems. It seemed to Ms. Jones that everyone was better off because of her lie. Johnnie had not been beaten, and she had not had to confront a violent and drunken father. Surely she had been right to lie. What else could she have done? And what could she do now to help Johnnie?

TWO WAYS TO THINK ABOUT ETHICS

Was Ms. Jones right in lying to Mr. Pugnacious? Let us assume a few things. Ms. Jones was right about the facts. Mr. Pugnacious would have beaten Johnnie. Moreover, he would have given Ms. Jones a bad time had she not produced Johnnie. She did indeed avoid some undesirable consequences. Does this decide the issue? Is it acting to avoid bad consequences or produce good ones that makes an action right? Or is it always wrong to lie? Ms. Jones strongly approves of honesty and deeply resents being lied to. Should she not treat Mr. Pugnacious as she expects to be treated by others? Isn't it always wrong to lie, even for a good cause? How would we decide?

We constructed this dilemma to illustrate the features of two major types of ethical theories—those that decide the rightness or wrongness of an action in terms of its consequences and those that do not. We shall refer to these as consequentialist theories and nonconsequentialist theories, respectively. Let us consider their basic features.

CONSEQUENTIALIST THEORIES
AND BENEFIT MAXIMIZATION

Consequentialist ethical theories hold that the rightness or wrongness of an action is to be decided in terms of its consequences. One way to understand consequentialist theories is to see them as committed to a principle that we will call the *principle of benefit maximization*. This principle holds that, whenever we are faced with a choice, the best and most just decision is the one that results in the most good or the greatest benefit for the most people. Thus the principle of benefit maximization judges the morality of our actions by their consequences. It says that the best action is the one with the best overall results. It does not directly tell us what is to count as a benefit or a good. That requires additional reflection. It merely says that once we know what is good, the best decision is the one that maximizes good outcomes. Thus, if Ms. Jones wished to decide on the merits of lying to Mr. Pugnacious by using consequentialist reasoning, she would have to balance the benefits and harms of lying against the benefits and harms of not lying. She would then choose the course of action with the best overall consequences. She would seek to maximize the good. But what is to count as the good?

To talk about the good is to talk about those kinds of things that are intrinsically valuable. What is it that makes something worthwhile for its own sake? One of the authors of this book is in the habit of going out and running a few miles over the noon hour. It is not something he greatly enjoys. Why then do it? There are several reasons. He needs the exercise, and he enjoys the company of those he runs with. But why value exercise? And why value others' company? In the first case, he is inclined to say that what he really values is health. Perhaps, in turn, health is valued because it allows him to do certain enjoyed activities such as canoeing and skiing. So running and exercise are instrumental values. They help him get what he wants and that is why he values them. Why value the company of other people? He just does, that's all. He does not run with these people because being with them is a means to some other end. He is not trying to enhance his professional opportunities or sell them something. He simply enjoys their company. Pleasant company, skiing, and canoeing, then, are the final reasons for his conduct. There is no "in order to" about doing them. They are intrinsic goods. That is, they are valued for their own sake.

A good consequentialist is not simply interested in producing any results that are intrinsically good. Consequentialists are interested in maximizing the good, that is, producing the most good. After all, it is relatively easy to produce some good results. Every gray cloud, we are told, has a silver lining. In fact, it is difficult to do something that produces no good. But the point is to choose that action that has the best set of consequences. If noon runs are to be justified, one must not only show that they produce some desirable consequences, but that the consequences produced are better than those consequences that would result from whatever else might be done. The good must be maximized.

Consequentialist theories can differ over what they consider good. The most influential form of consequentialism, hedonism, holds that the good is pleasure or happiness. But the Westminster Catechism answers the question "What is the chief end of man?" with the response that "The chief end of man is to glorify God and to enjoy Him forever." These are two different views about what the good is.

One of the most important varieties of consequentialism is a social application of hedonism called utilitarianism. This is a view of social justice developed in its most influential form by the English philosophers Jeremy Bentham (1748–1832) and John Stuart Mill (1806–1873). Its central doctrine is that social policy ought to be determined by what produces the greatest good for the greatest number.

How do we decide what counts as the greatest good for the greatest number? The starting point is the assumption that pleasure is good and pain is bad. If we want, therefore, to decide how well off any given individual person is, we must do so by measuring and adding up that person's total of pleasure and pain and by subtracting the total of pain from the total of pleasure. The result gives us a figure that is referred to as that person's utility. Deciding how well off a given society is is a matter of summing the utility of its individual members and dividing by the number of individuals in the population (providing, of course, that such things can be measured). This figure, known as the average utility, is a measure of general social welfare.

Deciding on the merits of a particular policy is a matter of determining its effects on the average utility. Those policies that produce the highest average utility are the most just. Thinking of moral problems from this perspective has the merit of reminding us that when we are evaluating the morality of an action or policy by judging its consequences, we must consider its consequences for everyone. If Ms. Jones is seriously to decide on the morality of lying to Mr. Pugnacious, she must consider all of the consequences for everyone affected. She must ask not only how her decision will affect her and Johnnie. She must ask such hard questions as whether her reputation as an honest person will be affected and whether any loss of respect for her truthfulness might not make her a poorer teacher. The other children in her class and in the school might also be affected by what she does. Utilitarianism requires that all of the consequences for everyone's well-being be taken into account.

Utilitarians sometimes disagree about whether the principle of benefit maximization should be applied to individual actions or to moral rules. Ms. Jones might reason thus: "The problem with asking me to decide whether it is right in this particular case to lie to Mr. Pugnacious is that I really do not have a very good idea of what the actual consequences will be. Perhaps I will save Johnnie a beating. But it is also possible that Mr. Pugnacious will find out that I lied to him. Johnnie might get an even worse beating then, and Mr. Pugnacious will never trust me again. I do, however, know that in the vast majority of cases the consequences of lying are less desirable than the consequences of truthfulness. Generally, honesty is the best policy. Since I am unsure of what the consequences of lying are in this particular case, I think I should do what I know is best as a general policy."

Here Ms. Jones has decided that it is better to apply consequentialist moral arguments to general policies rather than to individual actions. We should not have to decide whether or not to lie in each case. Instead, the appropriate question is whether a policy to permit or reject lying is best. Ms. Jones argues that it is easier to know what the consequences of certain kinds of actions are in general than it is to know what the particular consequences of a particular action will be. She might also have argued that it is dangerous to have people treat every decision as a case unto itself apart from any general rules of conduct. People are weak. Without the aid of moral rules they will do what is expedient, not what is right. And how can we have laws if we have to decide each and every case apart from the rest? Perhaps, then, it is moral rules or policies, and not actions, that should be evaluated.

Before moving on to consider nonconsequentialist arguments, we should look at two problems with consequentialism. One difficulty is that consequentialism, particularly in its utilitarian form, requires us to have information that is normally difficult or impossible to attain. Consider how difficult it is to compare pleasures or pains. Does good company produce more or less pleasure than good food? Is it worse to sit on a tack or receive a cutting insult? Utilitarianism seems to require us not only to be able to answer such questions, but to quantify them. Next, it requires us not only to know all of the consequences of our actions or policies, but to be able to judge the impact of these actions and policies for the overall distribution of pleasure and pain for everyone affected. It appears that moral behavior requires an omniscience that is unavailable to most of us.

A second difficulty is that utilitarianism can produce results that seem morally abhorrent. Let us imagine that a dozen sadistic people have had the good fortune to have captured a potential victim. They are debating whether or not it would be right to spend a pleasant evening torturing their captive. One of the group argues in the following way: ''We must admit that by torturing this person we will cause a certain amount of pain. But think how much pleasure we will give ourselves. And there are a dozen of us. While this person's pain may exceed the pleasure of any one of us, it surely cannot exceed the pleasure of all of us. Thus the average utility is enhanced by torturing this person. We ought to do so.'' Supposing these judgments about the consequences of torture are correct, do the moral conclusions follow? If one accepts utilitarianism, they seem to. Yet we suspect our moral sensitivities would rebel against such an argument. If utilitarianism can justify such actions, perhaps we should be a bit suspicious of it.

NONCONSEQUENTIALIST THEORIES AND RESPECT FOR PERSONS

A second way to think about Ms. Jones's behavior is suggested by another thought she expressed. Ms. Jones resents being lied to. Should she not treat Mr. Pugnacious as she expects to be treated by others?

This thought expresses a common moral idea. Its most familiar version is the Golden Rule, "Do unto others as you would have others do unto you." Might this thought not have something to contribute to the understanding of the problem?

Let us try to find out what additional ideas the Golden Rule contains by looking at it in a form offered by the German philosopher Immanuel Kant (1724–1804).[2] Kant's central moral precept is called the categorical imperative. "So act that the maxim of your will could always hold at the same time as a principle establishing universal law." This rather formidable phrase involves some less formidable moral ideas that express the content of the Golden Rule well. We will try to state the point more simply.

By a maxim or a principle Kant simply means a moral rule. "Do not kill" is an example.

What does it mean to say that a moral rule should be universal? Kant proposes a test to see if the principle underlying some action can be willed to be a universal law. If you are about to apply some moral principle to someone else, are you willing that it be applied to you in the same way? If you lie, are you willing to be lied to? If you steal, are you willing to be stolen from? If you are willing to lie but not be lied to, you are not willing that the principle that guides your behavior should be treated as a universal rule of human conduct. Kant has put in a more formal way what was implicit in Ms. Jones's reflection that she should treat Mr. Pugnacious as she would wish to be treated.

According to Kant, the Golden Rule requires that we act in ways that respect the equal worth of moral agents. It requires that we regard human beings as having intrinsic worth and treat them accordingly. That is why we have a duty to accord others the same kind of treatment we expect them to accord us. We shall call this idea the *principle of equal respect for persons*. The principle of equal respect involves three subsidiary ideas.

First, the principle of equal respect requires us to treat people as *ends rather than means*. That is, we may not treat them as though they were simply means to further our own goals. We must respect their goals as well. We cannot treat people as though they were things, mere objects, who are valued only insofar as they contribute to our welfare. We must consider their welfare as well.

Second, we must regard all people as *free, rational, and responsible moral agents*. This means that we must respect their freedom of choice.

---

2. Immanual Kant, *Critique of Practical Reason* (Indianapolis, Ind.: Bobbs-Merrill, 1956).

And we must respect the choices people make even when we do not agree with them. Moreover, it means that we must attach a high priority to enabling people to decide responsibly. It is important that people have the information and the education that will enable them to function responsibly as free moral agents.

Third, no matter how people differ, as moral agents they are *of equal value*. This does not mean that we must see people as equal insofar as their abilities or capacities are concerned. Nor does it mean that relevant differences among people cannot be recognized in deciding how to treat them. It is not, for example, a violation of equal respect to pay one person more than another because that person works harder and contributes more. That people are of equal value as moral agents means that they are entitled to the same basic rights and that their interests, though different, are of equal value. Everyone, regardless of native ability, is entitled to equal opportunity. Everyone is entitled to one vote in a democratic election, and every vote should be worth the same as every other vote. No one is entitled to act as though his or her happiness counts more than the happiness of others. As persons, everyone has equal worth.

When Ms. Jones proposes to apply the Golden Rule in deciding whether or not to lie to Mr. Pugnacious, she is not proposing to decide what to do by determining which act has the best consequence. Instead, she is trying to decide which action is most consistent with equal respect for persons. Theories that emphasize the principle of equal respect over the principle of benefit maximization are called *nonconsequentialist* theories.

Kant would wish to argue that all consequentialist positions will end up treating some persons as though they are means to the ends of others. When we seek to maximize the average happiness, are we not saying that we may trade the happiness of some for the happiness of others so long as the average happiness increases? When we do this are we not treating the happiness of those who are made less happy as a means to the happiness of others?

Thus Ms. Jones has another way to view her decision to lie to Mr. Pugnacious. She does not have to decide what action has the best consequences. She only has to decide whether her conduct conforms to the moral law—whether it can be consistently willed to be a universal rule of human conduct. She must treat Mr. Pugnacious as an end, not a means to someone else's well-being. Then she must do her duty. Ms. Jones, therefore, has a nonconsequentialist way of thinking about her behavior.

Let us consider two difficulties with this way of thinking. First, how can someone decide whether or not they are willing to have lying become a universal rule of conduct? Why is Ms. Jones unwilling to be lied to? What would we say to someone who argues that they are perfectly happy to have lying be a universal rule of conduct, that they do not care if they are lied to? Answers to such questions are soon likely to get us around to considering the undesirable consequences of lying. Lying cannot be accepted as a universal rule precisely because it has undesirable consequences. We cannot live with one another in peace if we are not usually honest. Such a turn of events poses a dilemma for nonconsequentialist theories. If they are unwilling altogether to consider the consequences of actions as relevant to their moral appraisal, it becomes hard to see how we could ever decide whether or not some moral principle could be universally willed. If, however, they are willing to talk about consequences, they will have to explain how they are different from any other consequentialist theory.

The second difficulty concerns how generally or specifically we should express the moral principle that underlies some action. Perhaps it is clear that we could not will lying to be a universal rule of conduct, but is it equally clear that we could not will lying in order to prevent the suffering of a child as a universal rule of conduct? How specific can we make our rules? If we must express them very generally, will our behavior not seem unresponsive to what may be very real and important differences in the circumstances under which we must act? If we can express them with considerable attention to circumstances, we reintroduce all of the vagueness into our choices that the categorical imperative seemed to offer hope of avoiding. Moreover, can a moral theory that makes the morality of an action depend on the generality with which it is described be reasonable? This seems an arbitrary matter for ethical judgments to depend on.

Let us summarize. Ms. Jones's assessment of her actions seems to rely on two quite different ways of thinking about ethical matters. Both seem plausible. Neither seems fully adequate. Can these views be integrated in some reasonable fashion? Can they be used as successful tools to think about the ethics of teaching? In order to address these questions, we will spend some time in the chapters that follow working through some quite real moral dilemmas that occur in teaching. We should try to see how we can look at each dilemma from the perspective of each theory. Perhaps then we can discover if there is really any objective way to address the ethical aspects of teaching.

We invite you to try out your own analyses and use of these theoretical perspectives on the following cases.

ADDITIONAL CASES

Truth or Consequences

Bayview High School, a racially mixed city school, enjoys the reputation of being relatively free from disciplinary problems. The administration is proud of the school and attributes this distinction to faculty cooperation and a system of communication that alerts the staff to potentially dangerous situations.

Recently, there have been some disturbances in the student body, and there have been some fights instigated by racial epithets. The staff, aware of these hostilities, was alerted to watch for weapons and other dangerous articles in the possession of students.

One Monday at lunch, Ms. Miller announced in the staff dining room that her wallet had been taken from her purse that morning. Twenty dollars was missing.

After classes ended that afternoon, Chico Diaz walked into the school store before leaving the building. He carefully took off his sweatshirt, checked the pockets, and placed it on a desk. He proceeded to the counter to purchase some school tee-shirts, notebooks, and pen sets. He produced a twenty-dollar bill as payment. Ms. Burner, the teacher in charge of the school store, noticed the bill, and she became suspicious. She went to the desk and looked in the pocket of Chico's sweatshirt, thinking that Ms. Miller's wallet might be there. What she discovered instead was a large switchblade knife. She placed the sweatshirt back in its original position and immediately summoned Mr. Marconi, the dean of discipline.

Mr. Marconi requested that Chico empty his pockets. When Chico did what was asked, the knife was discovered. Mr. Marconi, a strict disciplinarian, called in the principal, Mr. Lopez. Chico was informed that he was to leave the building immediately and consider himself suspended, pending a hearing on the matter the next morning with representatives of the school board.

Before the staff left the school, Ms. Burner was asked to visit Mr. Lopez in his office, and he asked her to be a party in the suspension hearing. Ms. Burner explained to Mr. Lopez that she had searched Chico's sweatshirt because she had been suspicious about another matter, not the knife. The knife had not been in sight. Mr. Lopez asked if Chico had seen her do this. When she replied that he had not, he said, "Good. At the hearing tomorrow you say that you saw the knife hanging from his pocket. That will satisfy the board."

There is a saying that the Bill of Rights does not stop at the schoolhouse door. In this case, it does not seem that Chico will receive due process, and Ms. Burner's search of his sweatshirt might not be legal. Chico does possess certain rights to privacy, as would any other citizen, and his treatment seems to be unfair. However, teachers and administrators have a responsibility to preserve the peace of the school and protect the other students. In this sense, an appeal to the general welfare is an attempt to justify the treatment that Chico is receiving. After all, he did have a knife.

Ms. Burner feels a bit guilty about the whole affair. She wonders if her search of Chico's clothing was the right thing to do. Now she is being asked by her superior to lie during the hearing. Chico has never been a very bad student, and she is afraid that the suspension is unwarranted and may have unforeseen consequences. What would you do if you were Ms. Burner?

Some Questions

1. Would you lie in this case if you were Ms. Burner? Why or why not? How is lying in this case similar and different from Ms. Jones's lie to Mr. Pugnacious?
2. Do both a consequentialist and a nonconsequentialist analysis of this case. Which seems more justified?
3. Which principle, benefit maximization or respect for persons, seems more important here? Why?

The Electrician

The consolidated high school of East Fork serves a large, sparsely populated area and draws students from as much as 20 miles away. Teachers often serve in more than one capacity to flesh out the functions of full staffing in the small school. Henry Trueblood teaches English, but he also assists in coaching football and track. Two years ago, when the full-time guidance counselor left, the principal asked Henry to take up some of that load in exchange for teaching one less section of composition. Henry quickly agreed. Besides having fewer poorly written themes to grade, he found that he rather liked helping students apply for college or land jobs in the local area. It gave him a different kind of satisfaction as a teacher—at least it had until now.

He had to make a tough decision about a reference. Tim Mulberry had never been a very good student. In fact, it was touch and go whether or not he would meet the minimum requirements for graduation next month. Tim was probably of average intelligence, but he never really applied himself at school. Henry now had him as a student in senior English. Tim handed in work late or not at all; he was sloppy and slapdash with his writing and at times Henry could not believe English was his first and only language. He had heard from other teachers that this was just Tim.

Still, Tim had had a hard life. More often unemployed than not, his father was in and out of the local jail for drunkenness and wife beating. His mother supported the family with a poorly paying job at the dime store and worked nights as a waitress. Tim received very little support and encouragement at home. He often got into trouble at school. Notes and calls to his home had little effect. Tim was within a whisker of failing English.

So Henry was surprised and delighted to find a letter on his counselor's desk informing him that Tim had applied to the union to become an apprentice electrician. Tim seemed to have some get-up-and-go after all. The letter asked for confirmation that Tim would graduate in June and a reference regarding his suitability for becoming an electrician.

Henry had a big problem. This might be Tim's only chance to learn a trade and lead a productive life. If he failed in his first attempt outside of school to make a go of things, he might give up altogether and join his father in the unemployment line. On the other hand, if Henry stretched the truth a bit, he might be obliged to pass Tim in English next month whether Tim deserved it or not. Moreover, Tim's work habits hardly seemed suitable to a trade in which mistakes could cause fire or shock in the homes and businesses of trusting clients. What should he do?

Some Questions

1. If you were Henry, what would you say in your response to the request of the electricians' union for a reference? Would you lie about Tim's work habits? If you just did not tell the union what you knew about Tim's undependability and carelessness, would that be untruthful? How would you treat the graduation issue?
2. Recommendations are requested all the time from employment agencies, organizations, prospective employers, and colleges. Should the records of students and opinions of teachers and counselors be made available to anyone who asks? The presumption of truth telling is essential to this process. Is that a realistic assumption?
3. How do the principles of benefit maximization and respect for persons apply in this case?

Chapter 2

Punishment
and Due Process

The NEA Code of Ethics contains the following statements:

> In fulfillment of the obligation to the student, the educator . . .
> 4. Shall make reasonable effort to protect the student from conditions harmful to learning or to health and safety.
> 5. Shall not intentionally expose the student to embarrassment or disparagement.

These precepts raise the issue of punishment. Punishment is often seen as a means of maintaining proper order and thus of eliminating conditions incompatible with learning and with a safe environment. Punishment can also subject the student to a risk of embarrassment or disparagement. What kinds of moral concepts are needed to discuss punishment intelligently?

A CASE TO CONSIDER

Mr. Fuse is the chemistry teacher at Middletown High. One day, while he was supervising a rather innocuous lab session, he was asked to report to the office to take an emergency call about one of his children. Noting that there was no possible danger in the experiment being conducted and that any really dangerous materials were locked up, he told his class to keep working and went off to take his call.

Mr. Fuse remembered two things about that day. The first was how relieved he was to find out that the "emergency" really was not one. The second was how panicked he became when he heard the explosion in the chemistry lab.

Running back as fast as he could, he entered the room to find it filled with smoke. His first concern was to discover if anyone was hurt.

No one was. Indeed, the students appeared to find it quite amusing. Whoever had set the explosion had set if off in a formidable metal wastebasket. There was little chance of anyone's having been hurt.

Mr. Fuse next noticed that one of the locked cabinets was open. He was certain that he had locked it. Someone, he concluded, had a key or was able to pick the lock.

Mr. Fuse considered the situation to be very serious. The student who had set off the blast may have had only the foggiest idea of what he or she was doing. The student might have erred and blown up half the school. Moreover, now someone had access to his supplies. There were things in those cabinets that, if mishandled, could be lethal. He thus began to question the class to find out who was responsible. He had no luck. It became apparent that many students had been doing their work and did not know who had done it. What annoyed Mr. Fuse, however, was that many students obviously did know who had done it. None of them were willing to point out the guilty person.

Mr. Fuse decided to punish the entire class. He gave them detention for a month and assigned them a thirty-page paper on the chemistry of explosions. Anyone who failed to do the assignment would fail chemistry. Detention, Mr. Fuse said, would be canceled when he found out who did it.

The next morning, Mr. Fuse found an anonymous note on his desk accusing a student named Alex of setting the blast. That made sense. Alex was bright enough to know what to do. Moreover, Alex was the school's most notable practical joker. Alex's popularity or his size, strength, and aggressiveness easily explained why no one would turn him in. The real clincher, however, was that Alex's father was a locksmith. All the pieces fit.

The only problem was that Alex refused to admit his guilt when confronted with the charge. That bothered Mr. Fuse a lot. He had only circumstantial evidence, and that was none too conclusive. Nevertheless, Mr. Fuse decided to punish Alex. The next day he announced that since the guilty person had been apprehended, he was lifting the class detention. Alex, however, was given detention for the rest of the year and a failing grade in chemistry. Mr. Fuse fully intended to make an example of him. He was responsible for the safety of his students. At all costs he had to make him understand that setting explosions was a serious matter. Being severe with Alex was a small price to pay for preventing a potentially terrible incident. No student hereafter would be able to think of getting into the chemistry supplies or setting an explosion as a harmless prank.

Has Mr. Fuse behaved fairly or justly? Let us consider first a brief argument for each side.

We may defend Mr. Fuse by noting that his first responsibility is to ensure the safety of his class. A dangerous situation has arisen. Someone has access to his supplies and seems willing to use this access to play practical jokes. Moreover, Mr. Fuse's class seems not to appreciate the seriousness of the matter. They regard it as humorous. Thus, it is quite reasonable to suppose that if something is not done there will be further incidents. Since the chemistry supplies contain materials that if mishandled can be life threatening, Mr. Fuse must take whatever action necessary to guarantee the security of his supplies and the safety of his students. His actions have very likely done that. At least he has demonstrated how seriously he views the incident and has shown his willingness to deal severely with offenders.

On the other hand, Mr. Fuse can be accused of dealing unfairly with both Alex and the entire class. Alex has been treated unfairly by being punished even though Mr. Fuse is not at all sure that he is guilty. Also, the punishment given to Alex seems inappropriate to the offense. Mr. Fuse has failed Alex in chemistry. Course grades, however, are normally based on knowledge of subject matter. Anyone who sees Alex's transcript will conclude that he failed to learn chemistry, not that he is being punished. Finally, Mr. Fuse punished some people he knows are not guilty to deter others from getting into the chemistry supplies. He punished the entire class even though he knew that most of the students had not been guilty and that many of them did not know who the guilty person was. Thus, Mr. Fuse can be accused of having done several unfair things. Before we begin to explore these issues in some depth, it may be useful to highlight several ideas regarding the use of punishment in schools. We offer the following imaginary dispute.

DISPUTE

A: As a teacher, I do not believe in punishment. It may be necessary in the world at large, but in school it serves no educational purpose.

B: But of course it does! Education cannot go on without order and peace in a classroom of learners. Could you imagine a school or classroom without any rules to govern behavior? Of course not! And if there are rules, there are sure to be infractions of them now and then. And if there are infractions, there must be provision for punishment or else there is no reason for students to obey the rules. Right?

A: Then you think that fear of punishment deters students from breaking rules. But obviously that is not true. Rules get broken no matter how harsh the punishment, and there is a limit to the harshness we can impose. Besides, fear may not be the best educational tool for teaching students to act properly. When fear of punishment does not deter, what is the good of punishing a student?

B: Well, you have to punish transgressors to give them their due. Justice demands it, doesn't it? I mean, if you knowingly act wrongly, you have to accept the consequences. It's an important lesson for students to learn about life and that is the educational purpose of punishment: to learn about justice.

A: But is it just to punish a whole class for the actions of only one or just a few members of the class? Teachers seem to do that all the time! Wouldn't it be more instructive to help students see that there are different reasons for following the rules and that some are better, more just than others? Fear of punishment is not as good a moral reason for acting properly as is respect for rules and laws or the sense of duty to do what society requires of its members. School rules are not made to underwrite punishment, but are necessary to maintain conditions appropriate to learning and safety, and students should learn that.

B: That may be true for some rules, but what do school dress codes and the like have to do with safety or learning or justice? I mean, are all school rules really essential to education or are some just forced on the young arbitrarily by an older generation? And what about the unjust application of rules?

How can students learn about justice when so often the innocent are punished by presumably just teachers and administrators who don't even give them a chance to defend themselves? There is no court of appeal, no jury system, no chance to challenge authority and present evidence in one's defense. Punishment is meted out directly and arbitrarily. Authority is not to be questioned. Justice is whatever those in power decree and decide.

A: You sound like you are on my side now. See how dysfunctional and uneducational punishment can be in school? As I said at the beginning, punishment serves no educational purpose that cannot better be served in more humane ways. Let's scrap punishment and teach good ethical reasons for right action.

B: But what do you do with the rule breakers? We really are back at the beginning!

CONCEPTS

One of the central ideas important in discussing punishment in schools and in the case of Mr. Fuse and Alex is that of due process. The general idea of due process is that people are entitled to procedures that ensure that decisions made about them are not arbitrary or capricious. Decisions are made arbitrarily when they are made without evidence. To find someone guilty of an offense without having sufficient evidence to ensure guilt is to behave arbitrarily. Decisions are made capriciously when they are made unsystematically or are based on irrelevant grounds. A judge who gives out significantly different sentences to people guilty of the same offense or who bases sentences on factors such as hair color behaves capriciously.

In order to prevent arbitrary or capricious judgments, free societies often insist that people who make decisions about others follow certain procedures that require them to confront available evidence and to base their decisions on it. Such procedures are commonly associated with criminal courts, but they are important wherever one person has the power of decision over another. A teacher who fails to read assignments carefully when grading, who gives tests that fail to measure accurately what the student can reasonably be expected to learn, or who assigns grades for reasons unrelated to learning violates important rules of due process.

In this case, Mr. Fuse can be accused of not following the kinds of procedures that are important in establishing guilt. He failed to give Alex a chance to defend himself, and he failed to tell Alex why he believed him to be guilty so that he could defend himself knowledgeably. Moreover, he relied on an anonymous note, having no idea of the reliability of its author. Certainly Alex had no opportunity to confront the person who accused him. Finally, Mr. Fuse failed to investigate the matter thoroughly. He did not attempt to discover who wrote the note; nor did he question other students to see if he could learn more about the incident. Instead, he convicted and punished Alex on weak circumstantial evidence.

Mr. Fuse also gave Alex a punishment that was inappropriate to the offense. First, the punishment was not chosen because its severity seemed appropriate to the severity of the offense. Instead, the punishment was chosen for its deterrent effects. Mr. Fuse did not ask himself what kind of punishment Alex deserved to get. He asked himself what sort of punishment would deter other students from doing something similar. Second, Mr. Fuse used a grade as a punishment. Arguably, grades are only properly granted on the basis of achievement. They are not suitable tools for punishment.

The final problem is that Mr. Fuse has punished the innocent. In this case, in order to deter future incidents, he gave an assignment and detention to the entire class despite the fact that he knew that some students were guilty neither of setting the explosion nor of withholding information about who had. He has been willing to punish some whom he knows are innocent to impress on all the seriousness of the incident and to make sure that the guilty are also punished.

Can Mr. Fuse defend himself against these charges? He might argue that some of his actions were regrettable, but necessary. He would have liked to have spent a few days investigating the matter more thoroughly in order to be sure that Alex was guilty, but it was important to act immediately before something else happened and while the incident was still fresh enough in the students' minds to allow them to profit from the example made of Alex. It seemed likely that Alex was guilty, and it was worth the risk of punishing someone who was innocent to prevent the possibility of a real disaster.

A similar argument might be given for the other objections. Perhaps a grade is not the best punishment, and perhaps there are difficulties in punishing the entire class; nevertheless, these actions were necessary to impress on the class that explosions were not a laughing matter. It was a successful lesson given in potentially dangerous circumstances. Mr. Fuse was merely taking seriously his responsibility toward the safety of his students. How could he forgive himself if his sense of fairness resulted in a serious accident, perhaps even the death of one of his students?

ANALYSIS

Let us look at these arguments from a consequentialist perspective. A consequentialist can be expected to have a reasonable regard for the idea of due process. After all, reasonable, conscientiously made decisions are far more likely to have desirable consequences than arbitrary and capricious ones. At the same time, a consequentialist is unlikely to treat rules of due process as absolute. Like any rules, they will produce different consequences when applied in different contexts. There will be cases when they ought to be laid aside. When following such rules produces potential danger or high levels of inefficiency, they should be modified or set aside. It is possible to place such high demands on public servants to justify their decisions that they cannot act. And it is possible to have such elaborate protections for the accused that it becomes difficult to convict even the guilty. The kinds of due process we provide must be determined by weighing the consequences of possible erroneous or unfair decisions against the consequences of failing to act decisively when there is a need.

If we are to decide about the kinds of due process to provide in cases of punishment, we must have some idea of what the desirable consequences of punishment are. Consequentialists have made three suggestions. Punishment may deter the individual punished or others from doing the same thing; punishment may help rehabilitate the guilty party; and punishment may separate a potentially dangerous person from society. In this case, we need not be concerned with the third of these ideas. No one has suggested suspending Alex from school; thus the issue is not raised. Nor was Mr. Fuse particularly interested in reforming Alex. The point of his actions was to deter future incidents. Is this a good reason for Mr. Fuse's behavior?

Here both of the earlier objections brought to bear against consequentialist arguments have some force. How does Mr. Fuse know what the consequences of his actions will be? Surely there are other stories to be told than his. If Alex is not guilty, the real guilty party may be emboldened to try again. Others, seeing that the probability of getting caught is small, may help. Some members of the class, seeing that Alex has been treated unfairly, may become alienated from school and become more prone to vandalism. This may occur even if Alex is guilty. Alex may become sufficiently embittered to do something unpleasant. In fact, the consequences of Mr. Fuse's actions are highly speculative and virtually unknowable. How can we determine whether he has acted correctly if we must know the consequences of his treatment of Alex and compare them to the consequences of treating Alex differently?

Even worse, it appears that consequentialist arguments have difficulty in giving a convincing reason why it is right to punish the guilty and not the innocent. In this case, it is entirely possible that punishing Alex will have deterring effects whether or not Alex happens to be guilty. If we are to judge punishment entirely by its consequences, why should we care if Alex is guilty so long as punishing him deters others from similar behavior? A possible response to this is that punishment is unlikely to deter people if they do not believe that the probability that they will be punished is related to their guilt. But this response misses the point. What it requires is not that the guilty be punished, but that it be believed that the guilty are being punished. What seems to be needed is some reason to believe that it is inherently right to punish the guilty and not the innocent.

A similar difficulty results if we consider the nature of the punishment. If the point of punishment is to deter improper behavior, then what is important about punishment is that it actually deter. Unfortunately this does not require punishment to fit the crime. It may well be that a severe punishment is required in order to deter minor offenses. Perhaps this is not always the case or even often the case, but again this misses the point. Consequentialism provides no reason why the punishment must fit the crime, and it can occasionally provide reasons why it should not.

Perhaps, then, we should ask how punishment might be thought of from a nonconsequentialist perspective.

The most common nonconsequentialist response is to hold that the point of punishment is to balance the scales of justice, ''an eye for an eye.'' Evil deeds are to be set right by inflicting pain on those who do them. Justice demands that evil be punished. Thus punishment is not intended primarily to deter further evil (although a nonconsequentialist may regard this as an added benefit); it is designed to provide retribution.

Viewing punishment as retribution explains why it is right to punish the guilty and not the innocent. Obviously, if the guilty person has not been punished, retribution has not been received. Similarly, the retribution theory explains why the punishment must fit the crime. If the retribution exceeds the evil, the scales of justice have not been balanced. The importance of punishing the guilty and of fitting the punishment to the offense explains the importance of due process. It is, after all, the provision of due process that permits us to be sure that we are in fact punishing the guilty in appropriate ways.

While it might seem odd to hold that this view of punishment is consistent with the principle of respect for persons, in fact it may be. We can only punish people who have done something morally wrong if we regard them as free moral agents who are responsible for their actions. Thus punishment can be seen as a way of regarding people as moral agents and as respecting their freedom to choose. If we see punishment as a way of people's accepting responsibility and retiring a debt of guilt, then we can also see it as a way of treating people as ends rather than means. Finally, it seems possible that guilty people might be willing to agree that morally wrong acts should be punished even when they are the objects of the punishment. Thus this view of punishment could meet the nonconsequentialist's test of universality.

From this analysis it would seem that Mr. Fuse will be able to make a better case for himself if he relies on consequentialist arguments. Perhaps the consequentialist case on his behalf is not foolproof, but the nonconsequentialist case that we have argued against him seems strong. Before we accept this conclusion, however, we should look at potential problems with the nonconsequentialist position.

Perhaps the weakest point in the retribution theory of punishment is the suggestion that the universe somehow requires that evildoers be punished with a compensating quantity of pain. Why should we believe this? The point can be put more forcefully. The retribution theory seems to require that we respond to one evil event by adding a second. How is the universe improved by adding an additional piece of suffering to it? If we are to punish evildoers, ought we not to expect some good to result? Otherwise, does not punishment merely add gratuitously to the pain in the world?

We might formulate this point in the nonconsequentialist's own value system. The underlying moral demand of nonconsequentialist views is that one recognize the value of persons as ends in themselves by showing them respect. How does it show respect for the worth of persons to cause them pain even when no good results? It is hard to see how inflicting pain on the guilty per se shows respect for their value as persons.

This argument provides another way of making the point that nonconsequentialist arguments tend eventually to display an interest in the consequences of actions in order to determine if they are ethical. It seems that it is difficult to decide whether or not to punish a guilty person without knowing if some good will result.

REFLECTIONS ON METHOD

Where does this leave us? We are not going to attempt to resolve either the difficulties of the case or the underlying philosophical arguments. These require long and serious thought. Before moving on to another issue, however, we would like to make a few observations about some of the conclusions to which we think these discussions point.

One conclusion that seems plausible at this point is that neither a pure consequentialist nor a pure nonconsequentialist view is likely to be successful. Consequentialist views seem capable of justifying immoral conduct in order to produce good consequences. Nonconsequentialist views seem to need to take consequences into account in order to be fully adequate. Perhaps, then, we need to see if there is any way to combine their best features.

Regarding the possibility of having objective ethical knowledge, there would seem to be good news and bad news. On one hand, we do seem to be able to conduct meaningful ethical arguments. It does seem possible to produce considerations that count for and against some ethical proposition. That at least suggests that ethical claims are not simply matters of taste. It is hard to know how to begin to have an argument about a matter that is entirely a matter of personal preference.

On the other hand, we have not been particularly successful in resolving any of the disputes we have raised. If we are going to succeed in showing that ethics can be an objective matter, we will have to show more than that such matters can be discussed. We will have to show that they can be rationally resolved.

So that the reader does not become too quickly discouraged, we would like to note that one reason that the case is difficult to resolve is that we have purposefully made it as morally ambiguous as possible. Its ambiguity makes it interesting and a good teaching tool. Its difficulty does not show that moral issues cannot be resolved or that thinking about ethics never gets us anywhere. Had we constructed a case in which Mr. Fuse had punished an innocent person, but which lacked some of the complexities of the current case, we believe that almost everyone would agree he had behaved unjustly. And we think that this conclusion could be successfully argued in both consequentialist and nonconsequentialist ways. We also believe that we could use the material in the discussion to show you that certain kinds of common practices in schools (such as disciplinary practices that punish an entire class because of the behavior of a few) are morally wrong. This case and many of the others we will give you are genuinely hard cases that involve conflicts between important moral principles. But not all cases are hard cases. Indeed, in our day-to-day lives, most of them are not. Perhaps many of our real moral dilemmas can be resolved by moral reflection.

We should add that many of the arguments presented have involved an appeal not only to reason, but also to an intuitive sense of the right thing to do. It seems intuitively wrong to punish an innocent person even if doing so produces good consequences. It seems intuitively wrong to punish a guilty person when there is no good to achieve thereby. These intuitions have been used as a kind of data against which ethical theories are tested.

Is this a legitimate strategy? It would seem important in answering this question to know what the source of our ethical intuitions is. Do we have some innate sense of justice that we must try to articulate fully? Do we know what is right when we cannot formulate the moral principle behind it in the same way that we know the proper use of a word even though we cannot define it? Perhaps we are blessed with insight into the nature of right conduct. Or perhaps our moral intuitions are formed by our training—the voice of our culture, so to speak, whispering in our ear.

These thoughts do not yet provide much assistance in our inquiry. Perhaps, however, they will be worth keeping in mind as we move on to issues of intellectual freedom. Before going on, you and your class might want to consider other cases of punishment and due process to get another perspective on this sensitive area.

ADDITIONAL CASES

A Graduating Senior

Nancy Smith is a graduating senior at The Day School, a well-established private school somewhere in the Northeast. She comes from a wealthy family and has just been admitted to an Ivy League college. Nancy is probably a nice girl deep down, but parental pressure has turned her into a sneaky and conniving student. Throughout her high-school career her teachers have complained that she is dishonest and manipulative. None of them were willing to give her an enthusiastic college recommendation, but she made the college she wanted anyway. She has complained about final grades on several occasions and has even questioned teachers' judgment.

Nancy took an elective English course in her last semester for which she did little work. Her teacher, Diane Jacobs, noted that Nancy often missed class but was excused by her mother for various reasons. Ms. Jacobs suspects that Nancy did not read the one book central to the course, *Pride and Prejudice*. However, Nancy submitted a final essay, comparing *Pride and Prejudice* to Dante's *Inferno*, that, according to every member of the English department, could have been submitted with pride in a graduate seminar. Ms. Jacobs is convinced that Nancy did not write the paper. Either she was given a great deal of help, or she plagiarized some of the information, or she plagiarized all of it. In any event, the entire English department is convinced that Nancy could not have written the paper. Many of them have taught her in other courses; some of them have accused her of plagiarism in the past. Nancy's paper contained many footnotes to *Pride and Prejudice* and the *Inferno*, but there are no references in it to any outside sources.

Ms. Jacobs had already met with Nancy several times. On one occasion Nancy was given a test on her own paper. She was asked to explain some of the statements made in the paper; she was also asked some simple factual questions about *Pride and Prejudice*. Nancy did quite poorly on these questions, reconfirming Ms. Jacobs's suspicions that Nancy neither read the book nor wrote the paper. More alarming, perhaps, was the indication from the test that Nancy had not read the *Inferno* either. Despite several opportunities to reveal her sources, Nancy has only mentioned some discussions with her sister's fiancé, a college student. She seems unwilling to concede that she had any help whatsoever.

Ms. Jacobs and the English department have brought the matter to the attention of the headmaster, Mr. Fitzgerald. They have presented the facts clearly and have demanded action on his part. They have recommended that Nancy not be allowed to graduate but that she be allowed to make up the course in the summer and, upon its successful completion, be granted late graduation. Mr. Fitzgerald has reviewed the case, remembering that Nancy has been a student at The Day School for thirteen years. He has also reminded himself that Mrs. Smith was just elected to the Board of Trustees. He does not need to be reminded that the Smiths are very wealthy people who might be making major future contributions to the school. Mr. Fitzgerald does not want to antagonize the Smiths if he can help it, but he does not want to alienate his teachers either. What should he do?

Some Questions

1. Do you think due process was followed in this case?
2. Do you think the punishment recommended fits the crime? Presumably other students have heard about Nancy's case. Should this have a bearing on Mr. Fitzgerald's decision?
3. Inevitably, in the real world, people of money and influence get special consideration. Although this is not fair, it might result in benefit maximization for an entire school, as in this case. Realistically, do you think such considerations are ethically warranted? Can you invent a case in which this point of view is persuasive? On what grounds might you object to such considerations even in the most persuasive case?

Beyond Word Processing: Whose Work?

Stearn High School is a public high school in an affluent northeastern suburban community with a national reputation for academic excellence for a comprehensive high school. It has regularly sent some 85–90 percent of its graduates to institutions of higher learning.

Dr. Dodge is a highly respected teacher of English literature and writing. He is a veteran teacher at Stearn with a reputation among students for being a tough grader. In fact, fellow professionals agree that a *C* from Dr. Dodge is a *B* from anyone else in the English department. He also believes that "writing is our finest product as the thinking species"; his students write, rewrite, and rewrite.

Michael is a junior in Dr. Dodge's class. He is a *B* student overall. He works hard, especially for Dr. Dodge, knowing that even with extra effort his *B* average could be lowered. Michael also feels some pressure from home; his parents have always been ambitious for him. They want him to get into the best college possible. Thus he has spent several hours every day for a week preparing a third draft of a final paper for Dr. Dodge and carefully addressing each and every comment from each of his two earlier drafts. However, his progress also has been impeded by his weak word-processing skills. He goes to his parents for help.

Michael turns in his third draft to Dr. Dodge. The general practice is that the first draft is reviewed first by a lay reader (an aide of some training) and then by the teacher. A second draft is then prepared, followed by a conference with the teacher if necessary. The third draft is almost always the final one. Dr. Dodge is stunned by the professional quality of Michael's final paper. He is stuck especially by the transitional paragraphs, often the bugaboo of students, in the twenty-four-page paper. He remembers that he worked hard with Michael on these bridges and that Michael had somehow resisted getting the idea of transition through his head. Therefore, the quality of this finished product surprises him. In fact, he seeks out the lay reader to review all previous drafts and commentary on Michael's work. To his dismay, he learns from the lay reader that in the district there are now some six word-processing consultants who, for a price, will also work with students in rewriting their papers. The lay reader will not divulge the names of any students who have used the service but says that, indeed, they have been used by members of the class. Dr. Dodge is convinced that no one can improve their writing that quickly; it is a long, long haul, taking years. He is especially convinced that the tricky and illusive transitional paragraphs cannot have come to Michael so quickly. Most importantly, his professional reputation and that of the school are now being challenged by word-processing services in the community that are willing to extend their services beyond inputting to actual rewriting.

Dr. Dodge decides to fail Michael for not doing his own work. He announces his decision in class as fair warning to other students not to avail themselves of the help of the consultants. Michael remains silent during the whole episode and is obviously embarrassed.

A week later, Michael's parents call the principal, Mrs. Perez, to tell her their story and demand that Michael be given a chance to rewrite the paper. They offer to guarantee that he will not use the services of the supposed word-processing consultant they had paid to help him sharpen his computing skills. They had not known that the consultant had also helped Michael write transitions. In fact, Michael told them that rather than helping, the consultant had acted more like a teacher, critiquing his inadequate transitions until he improved them himself. They demanded that the F be stricken from Michael's record and that an impartial member of the English department be selected to read and evaluate Michael's makeup paper. Dr. Dodge would then be required to substitute that evaluation for the F in computing Michael's final grade.

Mrs. Perez saw the justice in their request but felt uneasy about taking grading decisions out of the hands of the teacher giving the grades. She also worried about the availability (to those who could afford it) of computer consultants who helped students get better grades by providing writing services as well. Should she back Dr. Dodge or take the side of Michael's parents?

Some Questions

1. Obviously in assigning an F without even questioning Michael, Dr. Dodge did not seem to worry very much about due process. What might he have done to act more fairly? Is the alternative that Michael's parents suggested a good one? What about a teacher's right to determine a student's grade?
2. Is there any other way besides punishment to sensitize students to the problem of using consultants to do work that presumably is theirs alone? Should homework and paper writing be a solitary enterprise, or is it ever legitimate to seek the help of others?
3. Should Dr. Dodge be punished in some way either for being unfair or as a lesson to other teachers to be more fair in their appraisals of student work?

Chapter 3

Intellectual Freedom

A second group of statements in the NEA Code holds that the educator:

1. Shall not unreasonably restrain the student from independent action in the pursuit of learning.
2. Shall not unreasonably deny the student access to varying points of view.
3. Shall not deliberately suppress or distort subject matter relevant to the student's progress.

Students thus are entitled to some kind of intellectual openness. Why and of what sort?

A CASE TO CONSIDER

Mr. Lane looked at the page proofs for the article one more time. Eddie Ribald was a talented writer all right. Mr. Lane wondered how anyone with Eddie's sensitivity to words could have such a lack of sensitivity to people.

The article in question was a piece that Eddie had prepared for the *Springfield High Odyssey*, the school's literary magazine. Mr. Lane was the faculty adviser to the magazine.

Mr. Lane had to admit that Eddie's piece was marvelously written. It was so well done that Mr. Lane almost wondered if it was true. So would many students. Unfortunately, it was also so well done that no one could fail to recognize the characters. Eddie had their mannerisms and distinctive ways of speaking down so well that the fictitious names and the change of place would fool no one.

The story dealt with the seduction/rape of a high-school student named Sue Cross by a shop teacher named Alexander Wells. It spent most of the time analyzing Sue's feelings after the incident. Eddie described her anguish and despair and her drift into alcoholism with considerable feeling. Moreover, he presented Wells with some skill as a brutish clod who was incapable of caring how he hurt other people. Mr. Lane wished that he had Eddie's talent.

Nor was Eddie's story without socially redeeming value. Eddie had woven some interesting and well-developed themes about adolescent sexuality into the fabric of his story. And he had some important things to say about abortion. The story contained ideas worth considering.

Unfortunately, the similarity between the fictional Mr. Wells and the real John Waters, Springfield's physical education teacher, would be lost on no one. Nor could the similarity between Sue Cross and Beth Straight be missed. Springfield was a small school. Everyone knew everyone else.

Mr. Lane found it difficult to show much sympathy for Waters. He was a brutish clod. But it was doubtful that Waters was in the business of assaulting female students. He was not that stupid, and he did not seem to want for female companionship outside of school. Indeed, he had quite a reputation. But his penchant for humiliating the less athletic portion of the student body was well known. Less well known was his capacity for being rude to other members of the staff. Mr. Waters was something of a physical specimen who found an almost infinite number of ways to tell other men, both students and faculty, that muscles were what counted in life and that they were clearly inferior breeds.

Yes, Mr. Lane understood why Eddie would dislike Mr. Waters. He shared the feeling. Eddie was no athlete. No doubt he had come in for some painful moments at Mr. Waters's hands. Indeed, Mr. Lane suspected that that explained Eddie's story. It was very likely a piece of revenge.

His real concern was for Beth. It had taken him a while to understand why Eddie had picked her. Mr. Lane could not recall ever having met a nicer person. It was not that she was especially popular or especially attractive. It was just that she was one of the kindest and most gentle people alive. Everyone who knew her thought she was wonderful. It was almost unimaginable that Eddie could have some grudge against her. But, of course, that was precisely why she was chosen. How better to make Mr. Waters look bad than to make Beth his victim?

Mr. Lane was sure that Eddie had no conception of the damage that his story might do to Beth. Some students would believe the story. Even if they did not, it would not soon be forgotten. Beth would have to live with the humiliation for the next two years. The story was surely very cruel.

Mr. Lane had tried to explain this to Eddie, but Eddie simply could not be gotten to see that words could do people harm. Mr. Lane found Eddie puzzling. He was at the same time talented and tormented, brilliant and immature. Eddie wanted his revenge and was not going to see that it would have a high cost for Beth.

Unfortunately, Eddie was not only a good writer, he was also politically astute. He suspected that Mr. Lane might consider refusing to print his story, so he came to see him prepared with a truckload of arguments about freedom of the press and students' rights. He even managed to work some hints of lawyers and lawsuits into the discussion. Mr. Lane had to admire Eddie's ability to threaten him obliquely.

Mr. Lane did not wish to censor Eddie's story. He was a journalism teacher. He abhorred censorship. He had hoped that Eddie could be persuaded to be responsible about the matter. It would not have been too hard for Eddie to modify his story to make the characters bear no obvious relationship to real people. The role of the faculty adviser was to teach and advise, not censor. Nor did Mr. Lane wish to think about lawyers. If he decided to censor Eddie's story, he supposed that he would have to check out the matter before he did anything, but first he wanted to think it through on its merits.

Should he refuse to allow Eddie's story to be printed? He had never before censored a student publication. Prior to this incident, he thought that he could not imagine a case in which he would. But to refuse to do so would subject Beth to undeserved humiliation. Could he allow that? Mr. Lane decided to sleep on it. Perhaps his duty would be clearer tomorrow.

DISPUTE

A: In a free society, freedom of speech is a basic and inviolable right. You can't suppress or outlaw what people may say.

B: If that's true, what about laws against libel? Surely we have them to protect people from unjust public defamation of character.

A: That's different. I mean people should be free to say anything that doesn't harm other people.

B: Who is to judge if harm might be done? And what constitutes "harm" anyway? Are revolutionary ideas harmful to the status quo? Does sexually explicit language harm a reader or listener? Is telling someone the unvarnished truth about themselves harmful?

A: I don't know. I only know that the presumption of free speech is essential to openmindedness and to the truth's being heard. It's essential to have all views available so the best may emerge victorious. Suppression of ideas and opinions is the hallmark of a closed society.

B: But we don't stock pornographic books in school libraries, and we don't allow textbooks that are implicitly racist or antifeminist to be used in schools. In our society today, we obviously believe in censorship for the good of others and not in unbridled free expression. We do suppress some opinions and points of view.

A: It seems like that's true, but if the principle of free speech is compromised in that way, what's to stop anyone from coming up with a good protective reason to put down the publication of anything?

B: Nothing, I guess, if you are persuasive enough. Free speech isn't what it's cut out to be once you make exceptions, is it?

A: No. I still feel that it is essential in a free society, but I don't know how to defend it!

CONCEPTS

Let us look at some of the concepts that are used to justify intellectual freedom and are relevant to this dispute and the case of Mr. Lane and Eddie.

First, we should spend a little time examining the views of John Stuart Mill as expressed in "On Liberty," his classic essay on the subject. Mill summarizes his arguments for what he calls freedom of opinion in the following passage:

> First, if any opinion is compelled to silence, that opinion may, for ought we can certainly know, be true. To deny this is to assume our own infallibility.
>
> Second, though the silenced opinion may be an error, it may, and very often does, contain a portion of the truth; and since the general or prevailing opinion on any subject is rarely or never the whole truth, it is only by the collision of adverse opinions that the remainder of the truth has any chance of being supplied.
>
> Thirdly, even if the received opinion be not only true, but the whole truth, unless it is suffered to be, and actually is rigorously and earnestly contested, it will, by most of those who receive it, be held in the manner of a prejudice, with little comprehension or feeling of its rational grounds. And not only this, but fourthly, the meaning of the doctrine itself will be in danger of being lost or enfeebled, and deprived of its virtual effect on the character and conduct; the dogma becoming a mere formal profession, inefficacious for good, but cumbering the ground and preventing the growth of any real and heartfelt conviction from reason or personal experience.[1]

---

1. John Stuart Mill, *On Liberty* (Indianapolis, Ind.: Bobbs-Merrill, 1956), p. 64.

In this passage Mill constructs an argument for what is sometimes referred to as "the marketplace of ideas." The central contention is that truth is achieved or pursued by means of open criticism and public debate. Institutions such as free speech and freedom of the press are necessary if truth is to be sought and ideas improved. To censor an idea is to deny people the opportunity to consider it, to test their own views against it, and, thus, to learn. Moreover, uncontested ideas atrophy. People who hold to such ideas first lose their sense of the reasons for these ideas and ultimately of what these ideas mean. Uncontested ideas thus degenerate into meaningless clichés.

It may be worth noting that here Mill is speaking primarily about a social process whereby a society's ideas are examined, refined, and added to. Nevertheless, Mill also argues that freedom is important for personal growth.

Consider the following:

> He who lets the world, or his own portion of it, choose his plan of life for him has no need of any other faculty than the ape-like one of imitation. He who chooses his plan for himself employs all his faculties. He must use observation to see, reasoning and judgment to foresee, activity to gather materials for decision, firmness and self-control to hold to his deliberate decision. And these qualities he requires and exercises exactly in proportion as the part of his conduct which he determines according to judgment and feeling is a large one.[2]

Mill's point seems simple and compelling. Personal growth requires freedom. People who lack the opportunity to make their own decisions also lack the opportunity to develop the capacities to make their own decisions competently. Personal competence requires practice. When we deny to people the right to make their own decisions we deny them the right to grow.

These arguments make a strong case against censoring Eddie's story. To do so would be to interfere with the free marketplace of ideas. It would be to impose one's own judgment concerning what is true or correct upon the process of free exchange of information whereby free people can make such decisions for themselves. Granted that in this case someone will be hurt by publishing the story. But censors always argue that their censorship prevents some greater evil. To accept that argument is to accept the principle that people with power are entitled to impose their view of what is good or true on others whenever they think that it would be best to do so. Do not most censors believe themselves to be doing good? In addition, to censor Eddie's story would be

---

2. Ibid., pp. 71, 72.

to deny to Eddie the opportunity to be responsible for himself and to grow from his mistakes. The arguments for freedom that Mill provides seem to apply straightforwardly to this case.

Before we give the victory to Eddie too quickly, however, we should first consider another comment by Mill. Having provided his readers with a first formulation of his view of liberty, Mill adds the following qualification:

> It is, perhaps, hardly necessary to say that this doctrine is meant to apply only to human beings in the maturity of their faculties. We are not speaking of children or of young persons below the age which the law may fix as that of manhood or womanhood. Those who are still in a state to require being taken care of by others must be protected against their own actions as well as against external injury.[3]

Here Mill claims that the rights he argues for so forcibly for adults do not apply to children and others deemed not legally competent. Why? Generally, the answer is that the consequences of liberty for children are not the same as the consequences of liberty for adults. In the passage quoted, Mill notes that children need to be protected from the consequences of their own actions. Children presumably differ from adults in the degree to which they appreciate the consequences and the significance of their actions. They thus require protection from harmful and unforeseen consequences of their behavior. While Mill does not say so, it is reasonable for us to assume that he would hold that others are likewise deserving of protection from the actions of the immature.

Elsewhere Mill indicates that the benefits normally resulting from liberty do not accrue to the immature, who are not capable of profiting from free and equal discussion. Mill concludes that the immature may have their liberty interfered with provided that the end is their own betterment.

Thus, there is another side to the case. One might argue that Eddie's immaturity disqualifies him from fully participating in the right of a free press. Eddie lacks the maturity to understand the full significance of what his story might do to Beth. Moreover, it is doubtful that in this case the benefits that are supposed to flow from liberty will actually be realized. Springfield students are not likely to be led by Eddie's story to a better understanding of human passion and emotion. More likely,

---

3. Ibid., p. 13.

they are going to be led into a lot of ugly gossip and speculation about Mr. Waters and Beth. It is hard to see this as a case of people pursuing truth by means of free and equal discussion.

Nor is it obvious that Eddie will learn from his mistake. Perhaps he will, but it is also easy to believe that when he does he will wish that Mr. Lane had been willing to prevent him from his error. One can also easily imagine that Eddie will be harmed by his story's publication. Certainly many students will be angry about his treatment of Beth. If Eddie cannot handle Mr. Waters's ridicule, how will he deal with rejection by many of his peers? It is possible that the long-range consequences of publishing his story could be quite destructive to Eddie.

It is important to be clear about what really does follow from Mill's argument. Mill is not claiming that children never learn from discussion. Nor is he arguing that children never learn from being permitted to decide things for themselves. His point is not that children need detailed adult control in everything they do. Instead, his point is that adults are permitted to restrict the range of children's freedom for the benefit of the child, whereas such paternalism would be impermissible if directed toward adults. Adults have a right to freedom. They cannot be interfered with for their own good. Children are given freedom by adults when it is believed that it serves the interests of the child. Given this view, the question Mr. Lane must ask is not whether Eddie has a right to publish his story regardless of the consequences, but whether the consequences of allowing Eddie to publish the story are better than the consequences of censoring the story. Which decision will best promote the growth of the students at Springfield High?

ANALYSIS

Mill's argument is clearly a consequentialist one. It is based on the principle of benefit maximization. Indeed, Mill is quite clear in his essay that he will defend liberty on utilitarian grounds. He will attempt to show that liberty serves the greatest good for the greatest number. To a large extent the force of his defense of free speech and a free press depends on the suggestion that the utility of an idea depends on its truth. Simply put, true ideas contribute more to happiness than false ones.

Likewise, Mill's denial of liberty to those "not in the maturity of their faculties" is given a consequentialist argument. The reason the liberties of adults and children differ is that the consequences of extending liberty to adults and children differ.

The weaknesses of Mill's argument are also the weaknesses of consequentialist arguments in general. In order to know what to do, we must know what the consequences of our actions will be. But who among us really has a clear idea of what the consequences of allowing Eddie to publish his story will be? And how are we to judge the results of censorship?

Mill is willing to allow exceptions to his principles of liberty regarding children because of possibly undesirable consequences. Before we agree or disagree with this, we should consider that the argument may have broader application than to children. For example, in the mid-1980s there was extensive media coverage of the adulteration of some common over-the-counter medication with poison. This coverage generated several imitators and eventually cost consumers millions of dollars for the provision of tamper-proof packaging for many items. The consequences of this extensive publicity were quite foreseeable: There have been several similar cases. Moreover, the incident itself was local and hardly as newsworthy as the coverage received would indicate. Before the publicity, the chances of a similar happening elsewhere were slim. The scope of the coverage may have been dictated more by the desire to sell newspapers and television advertising time than by the desire to report significant news. In short, a case can be made that the news media behaved irresponsibly in giving the incident the kind of coverage it received.

One can find numerous other cases in which a free press seems hardly to serve the marketplace of ideas, but does serve commercial interests, often in ways that do genuine harm. Many parents use the television as a babysitter, with the result that preschool children are often raised on a diet of soap operas. The idea that current soap operas provide an important early model of family relationships is, we think, genuinely appalling. One could go on.

Do these abuses and misuses of the right of free speech make a case for censorship? A consequentialist is not committed to saying yes. It is worth noting, however, that the temptation to say yes is there along with the structure of an argument to defend the decision. The principle of benefit maximization tempts one to say that freedom is fine when it has desirable consequences, but not otherwise. Consequentialist ways of thinking can be a threat to liberty. Mill is very optimistic about the desirable effects of liberty, at least for adults. Suppose he is wrong. How much of our own liberty are we willing to forgo because liberty has different consequences than Mill supposed?

Consider a more imaginative, but perhaps more forceful, example. Imagine that in some future time a group of scientists announced that they had discovered a way to make all of humanity infinitely and permanently happy. All that was necessary was for people to turn themselves over to a hospital where they would have electrodes implanted in their brains that would stimulate their pleasure centers on a regular basis. Since they would be blissfully aware only of their own pleasure, they would need to be fed intravenously and would be confined to a hospital bed for the remainder of their days. People need not be concerned about this, however, since the system of maintenance is self-regulating and virtually foolproof.

The government, learning of this plan, did a quick calculation of the average utility and determined that since this plan maximized the happiness of everyone involved the plan would be compulsory. People would not be permitted to deny themselves their ultimate happiness.

The moral is that unqualified emphasis on benefit maximization, given the right facts, can lead not only to the denial of a basic right to freedom of choice, but to the substitution of happiness for growth. Suppose ignorance really is bliss. A consequentialist will prefer bliss.

On this topic Mill expresses the proper sentiment:

> It is better to be a human being dissatisfied than a pig satisfied; better to be Socrates dissatisfied than a fool satisfied. And if the fool, or the pig, are of a different opinion, it is because they only know their side of the question. The other party to the comparison knows both sides.[4]

This is the right thought. The difficulty is that it is hard to justify it with utilitarian arguments. Perhaps, then, there are other reasons to value freedom and human growth over and above happiness.

Let us look at the issue from a nonconsequentialist point of view. Recall that a central claim of many nonconsequentialist views is that persons are of value because they are moral agents. That people are moral agents who are responsible for themselves and their own conduct has much to say about these issues.

Most importantly, it provides a reason for freedom. If people consider themselves to be moral agents, responsible for their own conduct, then they must insist on the right to act as their choices dictate. To deny a person freedom is to deny that person the opportunity to be a moral agent. It is to fail to show respect for the dignity and worth of that person. People who believe that they are ultimately responsible for what

---

4. John Stuart Mill, *Utilitarianism*, reprinted in *The Utilitarian* (New York: Doubleday, 1961), p. 410.

they do cannot allow their choices to be arbitrarily interfered with. Nor will they willingly interfere with the choices of others. They will be willing to restrain others only when others interfere with their own freedom. Generally, however, they will insist on the greatest degree of freedom consistent with an equal amount of freedom for others.

Basic rights such as free speech and a free press can also be defended from this perspective. People who believe that they are responsible for what they do will also demand the conditions of responsible choice. They will insist that they not be denied information that is relevant to their choice, and they will want the opportunity to discuss and debate with others. Free speech and a free press are thus essential components of a society that regards human beings as responsible moral agents.

Personal growth is also an important component of moral responsibility. People who regard themselves as responsible agents will have to value their own competence. Responsible decisions result not only from freely available information, but from the wisdom and capacity to use it. Moral agents, thus, must value their own ability to make reasonable judgments and must as a consequence value their own growth.

Not only will such people value their liberty and growth, but they will not be willing to trade it for their happiness. People who believe that they are responsible for what they do will be unwilling to exchange their freedom for some other benefit, since this might result in their being compelled to do something that violates their moral duty. Part of the philosophical basis of the Nuremberg trials following World War II was the insight that moral agents cannot escape the responsibility of evaluating what they are asked to do. Obeying orders is never an excuse for a moral agent to do evil.

Does this shed any light on what Mr. Lane ought to do about Eddie's story? It might be argued that it does. The above nonconsequentialist arguments seem to make freedom more central to the moral life and prevent us from restricting another person's freedom merely because the consequences of doing so might be better; thus, Mr. Lane should let Eddie's story be published. But what happens if we apply the categorical imperative to the case of immature people?

If we were asked whether we were willing to make interference with other people's choices a universal rule of human conduct, we suppose most of us would refuse. Few of us would be willing to apply such a rule to our own case. We are not willing to be interfered with; thus, universality requires that we not interfere with others. But suppose we ask instead whether there are any conditions under which we might be willing to be interfered with. We might give a somewhat different response.

Most of us would be willing to be interfered with if our judgment was impaired. If we were sleepwalking and were about to fall down the stairs, we would wish to be interfered with. If we were drunk and were about to attempt a spin on the freeway, we would wish to be interfered with. Or if for some reason we were temporarily deranged and were about to commit murder, we would wish to be interfered with.

Moral agents will wish to be interfered with precisely in those cases where they are incapable of acting as moral agents. Competence is a prerequisite of responsible choice. We wish to be interfered with in just those cases about which we will later say that had we been in control, had we known what we were doing, we would have done something else. This is the sort of intervention in another person's choices that is consistent with equal respect for persons. Recall the suggestion that Eddie might eventually come to wish that Mr. Lane had refused to publish the story. This thought ought now to have a new significance. Might not Eddie, in a few years, come to view himself as having been very immature and as having been incapable at the time of fully realizing the significance of his act of vengeance on Mr. Waters?

Maturity remains a relevant consideration, but it has become relevant in a different way. The issue now is whether or not Eddie is in fact mature enough to be held responsible for his actions. Perhaps a good way to test one's insights into this question is to ask whether we are willing to treat Eddie as a responsible adult when it comes to taking the consequences for what he has done. If his story is libelous, are we willing to have him sued as an adult? If we are doubtful, that is reason to wonder if we are really sure that Eddie is adequately capable of a responsible choice.

The nonconsequentialist argument based on the principle of respect for persons is not problem-free. It shares with the consequentialist analysis the difficulty that the notion of maturity is vague. People are not simply mature or immature. Maturity is a many-faceted thing acquired over a long period of time. Any attempt to provide a legal definition will result in drawing a sharp line through territory without clear boundaries. It will be inherently arbitrary. This problem, however, is more severe for the nonconsequentialist. The consequentialist must ask about the consequences of allowing this person to make this choice at this time. These are not always easy questions to answer, but they are asked in a context in which there may be facts relevant to the answer. The nonconsequentialist must ask a more difficult question. It must be decided whether a person is sufficiently competent to be treated as a responsible moral agent. The considerable difficulty our society has with the insanity defense of criminal behavior should suggest the formidable problems involved. It is hard to see how to go about deciding how competent is competent enough.

Finally, an unqualified emphasis on respect for persons has the general difficulty of all nonconsequentialist arguments. It makes consequences irrelevant. Should we decide that Eddie is responsible for his behavior, must it follow that the effects on Beth of publishing his story are irrelevant? Would it not be better to find a way of balancing Eddie's right to be treated as a responsible agent against Beth's right not to be subjected to humiliation? Nonconsequentialist arguments seem to lack a way to account for how effects of behavior are relevant to their moral appraisal. That, however, seems counterintuitive.

REFLECTIONS ON METHOD

Let us conclude this discussion with these observations.

1. Note first that this debate is relevant not only to how we view issues of censorship and intellectual liberty, but also to how we see the basic objectives of education. Consequentialists will see education as a means of promoting the good, whatever they take the good to be. If the good is believed to be happiness or success, then consequentialists will see education primarily as a device to promote happiness or success. Thus, consequentialists are likely to have a rather utilitarian conception of the purposes of education. They will value human growth as a means to something else, as a means to promote the greatest good for the greatest number. Nonconsequentialists, however, will see education as a prerequisite to moral agency. It will serve to develop competent and morally responsible persons. Students will be encouraged to decide responsibly who they will be and how they will live with others. Education will be in the business of creating persons.

2. In this argument about freedom, unlike the previous one about punishment, neither moral theory seems to favor one choice over the other. It seemed clear that if Mr. Fuse was to defend himself, he would have to rely on consequentialist arguments. In this case, however, Mr. Lane might reach a decision to censor or not by arguing from either theory. Both moral theories have strong arguments for liberty, and both make maturity a consideration in whether liberty should be extended to children. Finally, both theories suggest reasons why freedom is an important component of an educative environment.

We should not conclude, however, that how we argue or what we decide is a matter of indifference. The basic values—educational values—of these two ways of thinking are different. Moreover, as we hope our imaginary future society will have suggested, these views can make a notable difference in some cases. Sometimes it is no small matter whether we should be willing to trade moral autonomy for happiness. They do not always go hand in hand.

3. Here, as in the previous case, we have not resolved the problem, and we have made frequent appeals to the reader's moral intuitions, again testing the moral theories against what seems to feel right. The results have been inconclusive. But we will have done more than simply test moral theories against intuitive moral judgments. Our deliberations will also have had some effect on what those moral intuitions were. Sometimes the analysis, if it was successful, suggested a new way of seeing the problem or showed that something unsuspected was involved in it. Thus, the moral theories and analyses not only have been tested against moral intuitions, but have actively restructured our moral intuitions and, perhaps, even changed them. This is another piece of evidence to keep in mind concerning the nature of moral reflection. Despite the inconclusive results, the process of analysis has not been powerless over our thinking and moral judgments.

Before going on to the next chapter, you may wish to examine some additional cases. The first one, "Censorship?", lends itself to role playing and developing an empathic understanding of heartfelt challenges to defenses of freedom. The second one, "Alternatives," raises the question of limiting a teacher's free speech.

ADDITIONAL CASES

Censorship?

John Corey is the principal of William Heard Kilpatrick Junior High School. He is a conscientious administrator, concerned about the welfare of the students and the quality of the curriculum. He is also an active participant in the meetings of the PTA, and he encourages parental interest in school affairs. He feels that he carries out his duties effectively and serves his institution well.

Mr. Corey's peace was abruptly disturbed one afternoon by an angry phone call from Mrs. Emma Lincoln, the mother of a student. Mrs.

Lincoln informed him that she, her husband, their minister, and several other parents had been monitoring the books that their children had brought home from school, and they were very unhappy with some of the selections from the school library.

As an example, she cited one book with which she was familiar, Kurt Vonnegut's *God Bless You, Mr. Rosewater*. This book, according to Mrs. Lincoln, is filled with stories of drunkenness, promiscuity, antisocial behavior, and irreligious thought. This, she said, is poor literature for her children to be reading and an inappropriate part of the school library collection. She added that many other books in the school library fit that same category. She and a committee of concerned parents planned to raise this issue at the next meeting of the PTA. They would demand that the school library collection be reviewed and that these books and other objectionable items be removed. If necessary, they would take legal action. It was their right as parents and taxpayers.

That this issue had arisen among the parents was a complete surprise to Mr. Corey. His first thought was to call Mrs. Jennings, the school librarian. Christine Jennings had been with the school for thirteen years, had compiled most of the book collection, and was a valued member of the staff. She had a reputation for being conservative in social matters and was acquainted with many of the parents. She would know how to placate them.

Mr. Corey was shocked by her angry response and flat rejection of the case presented by Mrs. Lincoln. In Mrs. Jennings's view, *God Bless You, Mr. Rosewater* was a minor classic of recent American literature that should be included in any school library. It celebrated human frailty, the humble civic virtues, and the possibility of kindness in an unkind world. According to Mrs. Jennings, it was this sort of work to which the students ought to be exposed, and she would make this argument in favor of any book the parents might select from her library. That her handling of the library would be questioned at all was a personal insult she would not accept. Furthermore, in her opinion, no group had the right to censor a library, and she was prepared to fight in defense of that position. With that, she hung up the telephone.

Mr. Corey gently replaced the receiver in its cradle. Much had happened in a brief part of the afternoon. An issue had arisen that could seriously disrupt the peace of the school and extend beyond its walls. A group of parents was up in arms, and his librarian had wrapped herself in the Bill of Rights. It was his responsibility to salve the anger of the parties in this dispute, yet still carry out his duties as principal. Mr. Corey had no strong opinion about the books in question, but he had to arrange a compromise. The next PTA meeting was a week away.

The meeting only exacerbated the problem. The parents had planned their strategy and presented a united front. The Reverend Campbell, the Lincolns' pastor, served as their spokesman. He presented a list of titles that the group found to be offensive, including Vonnegut's *God Bless You, Mr. Rosewater* and *Slaughterhouse Five,* Joseph Heller's *Catch-22,* and J. D. Salinger's *The Catcher in the Rye.* The Reverend Campbell claimed that these books were obscene, un-American, and, in an insidious way, introduced a secular humanism into the school. The parents had the right to protect their children in such matters and make their opinions felt. It was their demand that such books as the parents' committee might select be removed from the library and that they have the right to review the place of such works in the school curriculum.

Mrs. Jennings spoke for herself and a number of the teachers. It was their position that parental intervention in the library or the school curriculum would be censorship, a violation of academic freedom. Such a situation would indeed be un-American. They would stand for no interference.

No dialogue developed, and the meeting became a shouting match. Mr. Corey called an adjournment and promised that he and the school board would attempt to reach a compromise on the issue.

After much discussion, Mr. Corey and the school board submitted a possible compromise to a later meeting of parents and teachers. The provisions of the plan were:

1. No books would be removed from the library, and no changes would be required in the curriculum at that time.
2. A parent could request, in writing, that a student be prevented from taking certain books from the library.
3. If the parents found a certain work to be offensive, the student could be excused from the assignment and allowed to leave the classroom.
4. A committee of concerned parents and teachers would be created in order to review new acquisitions for the library and recommend any changes in the curriculum.

Both parties rejected the compromise. The Reverend Campbell stated that the proposal did not resolve the original problem and avoided very real moral issues. He could not sanction the presence of books in the library that were morally objectionable. It was his duty to protect all the students, not just a few. Furthermore, the parents who chose to participate in the new program would subject their children to the implied criticism of their teachers and the ridicule of their classmates. This would be harmful and uneducative for the students. The

Reverend Campbell announced that the parents intended to file suit against the school board and were willing to keep their children out of school unless the principal removed the objectionable books from the library. They would elect a more compliant school board, if necessary.

Mrs. Jennings charged that the new plan only served to establish a form of censorship. It was the teachers' position that the Reverend Campbell and his group had no right to impose a single point of view on a public institution. The school board's proposal was an insult to the librarian's taste and the teachers' professionalism. They would not abandon their legitimate control over the classroom and yield to outside pressure. The teachers were prepared to file a countersuit against the parents and might even strike to protect their academic freedom.

What can Mr. Corey do in order to help resolve this problem?

Some Questions

1. Try role playing this case. Imagine a public meeting where all the major characters plus some students and teachers are allowed to present their points of view. After all have spoken, analyze each argument to see what principles are being used to justify a position. Which arguments seem to have the most merit? Why?
2. Write a plausible ending to this case. Compare your ending with that of others. Do all of these endings occur in real life? What factors might make the most desirable ending most probable?
3. The problem of the maturity of students is a constant one for teachers. Can you formulate any standards, principles, or rules that might help teachers make finer judgments about what is and is not appropriate material for students of different school or grade levels?

Alternatives   *Senior Slump*

The idea of an alternative school is not a new one, but this was the first time Marple Grove was trying to use it to solve the persistent problem of senior slump. Once students found they were accepted into a college, especially after early decisions, finishing the year of regular high school work was not particularly appealing.

Everyone went through the motions, with some exceptions. A few were so lax they found themselves failing a required subject, and there were some close calls at graduation. Most, however, just coasted, including the teachers. It was just an accepted part of the school culture at Marple Grove.

Last year, however, a small group of teachers found themselves wondering about the waste of time and talent, their own included, that resulted from senior slump. Wouldn't it be more educationally beneficial if they could provide an alternative to work as usual in their regular classes for those who had applied to college, an alternative school within a school that was educationally sound and yet different enough to be interesting and challenging?

They put their heads together and came up with an exciting proposal that they presented to Mrs. Zinna, the principal. It was unusual, but with careful structuring and monitoring, it would meet state requirements. Mrs. Zinna felt strongly that it was worth a try. She invited the two teachers who had emerged as leaders of the group to present the plan to the school board.

They convinced the board that a carefully controlled, educationally safe, and thoroughly accountable experiment with the alternative school plan was worth a try. An experimental program was approved, with the proviso of careful reviewing and revoting at the end of two years.

Ms. Winsome and Mr. Losesome were the two lead teachers. A year had passed, and things seemed to be going well for the twenty students selected for the experiment. The parents were pleased with the serious involvement of their sons and daughters in the program. The teachers felt they had really found the solution to the problem. The students enjoyed being treated differently and having an unusual curriculum for their last half-year.

Ms. Winsome felt it was a waste of time to wait another year before making the alternative an opportunity for all seniors, not just a few. She went to Mrs. Zinna to try to persuade her, but the principal took her promise to the board and her integrity as an administrator-researcher as reasons to stay with the original plan. Hard evidence of success, based on successful replication the second year, was a better basis for approving the program for all students than the intuitions and subjective judgments of a lead teacher. Mr. Losesome agreed with Mrs. Zinna.

Ms. Winsome was fit to be tied. She knew in her bones that she was right. It was not fair to deny the entire next senior class what clearly was a better kind of education. However, she knew it would be wrong to go over Mrs. Zinna's head to the board herself. It seemed like such a waste, though.

Then an idea hit her that seemed to provide the solution. After all, free speech and freedom of the press were principles she and other social studies teachers extolled all the time. She would write a letter to the local paper as an individual citizen reporting on her very positive feelings about the alternative school and urge other concerned citizens to petition the board to make it a regular and full part of the high school program next year.

This was a perfect solution! She even fantasized that groups would come to the board meeting to present their own ideas; and in that "free marketplace of ideas," the truth would win out more quickly than in some closed and narrow experimental process. She saw herself as a free citizen acting responsibly in her community and serving the public good. She lifted her pen and began, "To the Editor . . . "

Some Questions

1. Can you think of situations or circumstances in which the free speech of teachers in their role as professionals should be curtailed? When do individual rights give way to professional obligations? Do you think Ms. Winsome did the right thing?
2. Look at the NEA Code. Is there any provision in it relevant to this case? Do professionals have special obligations to other professionals?
3. Is there a clash between the process of a free marketplace producing truth and experiment producing truth? In this case, are we most concerned with moral truth, scientific truth, or educational truth? Are these different things with different processes for arriving at them?

Chapter 4

Equal Treatment
of Students

The NEA Code also holds that the educator:

6. Shall not on the basis of race, color, creed, sex, national origin, marital status, political or religious beliefs, family, social or cultural background, or sexual orientation, unfairly:
   a. Exclude any student from participation in any program;
   b. Deny benefits to any student;
   c. Grant any advantage to any student.

A CASE TO CONSIDER

Mrs. Andrews could tell from the crash at the back of the room that Tim and Paul were at it again. Never had she seen a more perfect hatred. The boys had seemed to despise one another from the first day of class. Mrs. Andrews recalled that they had gotten into a fight on the playground before school had started. Here was true animosity at first sight. Each was a red flag to the other's bull.

Nothing she tried worked. She reasoned with them. She threatened them. She bribed them. She talked to their parents. She had even sent them to the school psychologist. Perhaps that was why he had resigned. There was only one thing that worked. They had to be kept occupied as far from one another as possible.

That had its drawbacks, too. The basic problem was that they were nearly identical in their ability. They were slightly below grade level in almost everything. Mrs. Andrews recalled that in physics oppositely charged particles attracted one another and like-charged particles repelled. Whoever discovered that obviously had met Paul and Tim. How could she have them both in the same reading group, in which both seemed so clearly to belong? When they were within reach—or even sight—of one another, reading time was over. They had even disrupted her other reading groups last week. When she was working with another group, that meant that they were together somewhere else in class—out of sight, but unfortunately rarely out of hearing for long. Mrs. Andrews wished longingly that King Elementary School had enough students to have two fourth-grade classes; then she could make a trade to solve the problem.

She decided to try putting the boys in different reading groups. That made things better. She remembered that there had been peace in the class for almost a week last month when she had assigned Tim to the lower reading group and kept Paul in the middle group. Everyone got a lot more work done.

There was one problem with that arrangement, however. It was terrible for Tim. He obviously felt demoted and stopped working. Moreover, the material in his new reading group was too easy for him and he quickly lost interest. Mrs. Andrews could see him in the reading area of her room while she was working with another group. He was staring off into space. Perhaps that was better than fighting with Paul, but Mrs. Andrews was not sure.

Mrs. Andrews had also thought of putting Tim in the highest reading group, but she was almost sure that would not help. Tim just could not make it there, and she did not want to subject him to demoralizing failure.

The final alternative to consider was moving Paul to the lower group and Tim back to the middle group. Mrs. Andrews, however, had no reason to believe that Paul would respond any better than Tim. Putting children in the wrong group was simply unfair.

Mrs. Andrews had another reason for not wanting to try the experiment with Paul. Paul was black. Somehow she was reluctant to take a risk with the progress of a minority student. Also there were possible complications. Racial peace had reigned in King school for almost five years now. Indeed, in the elementary grades children were becoming used to the idea of an integrated school and had begun to pay little attention to the color of their classmates' skin. Mrs. Andrews doubted that Paul and Tim paid much attention to the tones of the skin they punched on. Their hatred ran deeper than race.

Mrs. Andrews was happy about the comparative racial harmony in the school and wished to do nothing to disturb it. She worked hard to make sure that everyone was treated the same. Normally she was pleased to find that ability grouping did not produce segregated reading groups. Unfortunately, if she put Paul in the lower group, that would make the middle group entirely white. Parents and children would notice. People were still suspicious and watchful. Mrs. Andrews did not want segregated reading groups if she could help it. Nor did she want to appear to be punishing Paul, but not Tim.

Another crash brought Mrs. Andrews back from her momentary reflections, and she moved off to apprehend and chastise the malefactors. A permanent solution would have to wait for another day.

DISPUTE

A: We should all be treated equally. That's what justice and fairness demand. Ethical educators must make equity one of their central decision-making principles.

B: But do we in education really treat people equally? We pay the superintendent more than the teachers. We give some students A's and others D's. We provide free compensatory education to the culturally deprived. We give special educational opportunities to the gifted. It seems that just the opposite is true!

A: It's only true if you think equal treatment simply means the same treatment for all regardless of relevant differences. Superintendents get more pay because they have greater responsibility than teachers. Students receive A's because they have reached a higher level of achievement than D students. Equity and fairness demand paying attention to those differences that make a difference.

B: So equal treatment isn't important. Differences are?

A: No, I didn't say that. Equal treatment is essential in two ways. We must presume people are to be treated equally, and we should treat them so unless some relevant difference exists. Second, all those who have the relevant difference, such as doing A work, should be treated equally. You can't give one a B and the rest A's if their work is of equal quality.

B: I'm a little mixed up. You mean equality counts unless there is a difference, and then treating people differently is okay as long as you treat them equally?

A: Precisely!

B: I feel like I'm playing "Who's on first?" Let me try this a different way. Let's take the compensatory education and gifted examples. Let's suppose that there are differences that make a difference and that within each group equal treatment is given. Is it just, is it fair to take limited educational resources away from others to give to these groups? Why should those who aren't gifted have to give up some of the educational benefits they might have gotten so that those so much more naturally endowed could have more? That seems like inequity of the highest order!

A: I notice you didn't say anything about compensatory education. Doesn't justice demand that we give to those who have been deprived a chance to catch up with others, give them an equal chance to benefit from an education so they can become the real equals of others?

B: Yes, that seems fair. It's like taking from the rich to give to the poor. But supporting gifted education seems more like taking from the poor and giving to the rich! How can you justify that?

A: Benefit maximization! The gifted are society's greatest human resource. They are our future doctors and medical researchers, our scientists and engineers, our educators and political leaders. In the long run, given the best education, they will improve the lives of all of us the most.

B: I'm still confused. How do you know when a difference really makes a difference that is ethically acceptable?

CONCEPTS

Is it just to treat Tim and Paul differently? Let us start with a consideration of two aspects of the case. First, Mrs. Andrews has one option that consists of trading Tim's progress in reading for the peace and progress of the entire class. She might argue that everyone is better off under such a trade except Tim. The gains outweigh the losses. Second, Mrs. Andrews seems to be more willing to impose a costly solution to the dilemma on Tim than on Paul because Paul is a minority student. Is Mrs. Andrews right in being more sensitive to the needs of a minority student, or is this a form of reverse discrimination?

The question is one of justice in distributing educational resources. How are such problems thought about? Let us start with a definition of justice proposed by Aristotle (384–322 B.C.). Aristotle held that justice consists of treating equals equally and unequals unequally.

What Aristotle meant by treating equals equally is that people who are the same vis-à-vis some relevant characteristic are entitled to be treated in the same way. For example, if high school grades are the basis of admission to a university, then two people with the same grades should receive the same treatment. Either both should be admitted or both should be rejected.

The other side of the coin is to recognize that when people differ on some relevant characteristic they should be treated differently. A visually handicapped student is not being treated fairly by being given the same book to read as a sighted student. Here fairness requires different treatment. Each student should receive reading material from which that student can profit. That requires different kinds of reading material for the visually handicapped.

Note that these ideas generate two kinds of questions that we must be able to answer if they are to be sensibly applied. First, we need to know what is to count as a relevant characteristic. Intuitively, so far as education is concerned, it seems as though such things as a student's abilities, needs, and interests are relevant differences. On the other hand, race and sex would seem to be irrelevant. But how do we know this? Are exceptions possible?

Some of us would find it plausible to treat sex as a relevant characteristic so far as physical education is concerned, although we also suspect that we could generate a hot debate about exactly how or why it is relevant. Can race ever be relevant? Again, we may find agreement on the general proposition that race is a relevant consideration when we are trying to provide remedies for racial discrimination. Here, too, agreement on specific cases is less likely.

The question of whether Mrs. Andrews is discriminating on the basis of race because she is more willing to impose a cost on Tim than on Paul is essentially the question of whether race can ever be a relevant consideration in how people are treated. Is it possible, for example, that Paul may be a victim of racial discrimination? Could we argue that Mrs. Andrews ought to be especially careful about treating Paul fairly because of the history of discrimination against blacks in the United States? Does a history of discrimination against blacks make Paul a victim because he is black, or must Paul himself have been discriminated against?

The second major question raised by Aristotle's concept of fairness is how treatments are linked to relevant characteristics. Let us assume for the moment that differences in ability are relevant to the kind and quantity of education a person receives. How do we decide what kind of education to provide people who differ in ability? We might argue, for example, that students with low ability deserve more educational resources than students with high ability because they need them more. On the other hand, we might also argue that students with high ability should receive more educational resources than students with low ability because they will be able to do more with them. A prudent investment of resources will put them where they will do the most good.

This question leads quickly to the issue of how we are to balance competing claims for educational resources. Educational resources are not infinite. People cannot have all of the educational resources they want or need. How, then, are we to choose? We cannot just look at people in isolation. We cannot simply say that because this person has a certain characteristic he or she deserves a certain kind of educational treatment. Such a way of thinking would be possible only in a world where needs were never in conflict. In our world, we can never decide what one person is entitled to without balancing that person's claims against those of others.

The question of whether Tim might be misclassified for the sake of the welfare of the entire class fits here. Tim and Paul are equals. The case was constructed to ensure that there were no relevant grounds for treating them differently (except possibly for race). Nevertheless, in order to know that Tim would be treated unfairly if he were assigned to an inappropriate reading group, we have to know how to decide how characteristics people possess are related to the kind of treatment they deserve. How do we know that the lower reading group is inappropriate for Tim?

The heart of the issue is that we need to know whether it is ever appropriate to trade one person's welfare for that of the group. In order to decide this, we need to have some principled way of balancing competing claims. When needs conflict, how do we decide who gets what?

ANALYSIS

Consequentialist views provide some quite straightforward ways to analyze these issues. Reasoning from the principle of benefit maximization will start from the conviction that decisions about how resources are to be allocated must be made in terms of what promotes the greatest good for the greatest number. What distribution of educational resources will enhance the average welfare? The answer to the question of whether it is permissible to trade the welfare of one student for the welfare of the group is therefore clear. Such trades are not only permitted, they are required as long as the average welfare of the class is promoted thereby. Peace in the classroom is worth the price.

Benefit maximization can also give an account of relevant characteristics and of how we know that a given treatment is appropriate to persons possessing such characteristics. Consider, for example, how a utilitarian might reason about race. Race will not be considered as a relevant characteristic because race has nothing to do with the use that a person can make of an educational opportunity. To make opportunities available on the basis of race is, therefore, to distribute them in a far less efficient way than they would be distributed were we to use the criterion of ability to profit.

Ability to profit, however, is clearly a relevant characteristic. When we allocate educational resources on the basis of ability to profit, we are putting them where they will do everyone the most good. We admit intellectually talented people to medical school, for example, because we believe that they make better doctors than those who are less talented. We all benefit from improving the quality of the medical profession. We do not admit people to medical school on the basis of race because race is unrelated to a person's ability to profit from medical instruction and to become a good physician.

Consequentialists are not likely to be impressed with the argument that minorities ought to be given preferential treatment in admissions or in any other distribution of educational resources because they have been the victims of injustice. It is the future, not the past, that is relevant to consequentialists. The question is not how a person came to have those characteristics to which educational benefits are to be attached. It is who has those characteristics that indicate that that person will make the most profitable use of the opportunity. When reasoning from the principle of benefit maximization, the past is morally irrelevant. It is the future that counts.

Consequentialists may, however, be moved to consider race as a relevant characteristic for future-oriented reasons. For example, if preferential admissions will enhance the diversity of a student population to the benefit of everyone or if it will improve the quality of minority medical services, consequentialists may approve of preferential admissions. To be able to identify some characteristic as a relevant characteristic, a consequentialist needs an argument that shows that using that characteristic in a decision results in beneficial consequences.

If Mrs. Andrews were to reason as a consequentialist about her dilemma, she might argue as follows: "First, I must separate these boys. They cannot be in the same group together. Therefore, I will have to move one of the boys to an inappropriate reading group, since the entire class will be better off as a consequence. The trade between the welfare of one child and the welfare of all is necessary. Moreover, I should choose to move Tim. If I move Paul, that may serve to undercut the trust that has been built up between black and white students and may generate concern among black parents that their children will not be treated fairly. By choosing Tim rather than Paul, I will avoid some significant undesirable consequences. So, I will assign Tim to the lower reading group."

Let us consider some objections to this analysis. First, we need to think a bit more about the trade that Mrs. Andrews is proposing. Tim is going to be required to sacrifice the quality of his education for the benefit of the entire class. What are the limits on such a trade? How much could Tim be asked to sacrifice? The answer that follows from benefit maximization is simple. Tim may be deprived of his education to any degree as long as his loss is outweighed by the gains to the rest of the class. Indeed, if it turned out that the average welfare of the class was enhanced by excluding Tim entirely, the principle of benefit maximization not only permits this, it requires it.

Consequentialism thus seems to have no way of limiting the extent to which the welfare of one can be traded for the welfare of all. Intuitively, however, it seems that there ought to be some limit to the extent to which Tim might be deprived of an education. Does Tim not have some basic right to an education that cannot be violated for the benefit of others, no matter what?

It is tempting here to try to see Tim's loss as a punishment for his bad behavior, but this does not help. Tim is too young to be held fully responsible for his behavior. Moreover, even if we do think of his misclassification as a punishment, we have essentially the same problem. What are the limits to the punishment? In this case, there is no attempt to fit the punishment to the crime. The only issue is what enhances the average welfare of the class. Furthermore, the fact of Tim's misbehavior is really quite irrelevant to how consequentialists think about such cases. Even if Tim were entirely blameless in the matter, consequentialism would require the same trade as long as it produced the same results. We are still left with the question of whether Tim does not have some right to an education that could not be traded for the welfare of the group.

A second difficulty is that consequentialism does not take history into account. History often seems important in our moral deliberations, however. History is particularly important when we need to consider the remedy for prior injustice. It often seems morally appropriate to give someone something that they do not otherwise deserve if their current lack is a consequence of some prior injustice.

Consider a simple illustration. Suppose we have two candidates, Smith and Jones, competing for the same position. Suppose also that we know the following about them. First, both are capable of doing the job. Second, Smith is more qualified than Jones. Third, Jones was the victim of discrimination in his pursuit of his qualifications. Finally, had Jones not been discriminated against, he would have been more qualified than Smith. Who is entitled to the position?

The consequentialist may argue that Smith is. Smith is currently more qualified than Jones. Thus, he will put the position to better use, and we will all be better off as a result. This is to say that consequentialism does not consider as relevant the history of how these qualifications were obtained. The only question asked is what these qualifications mean for future performance. Might not one argue, however, that Jones, not Smith, is entitled to the position? Jones would have been most qualified had he not been discriminated against. Jones has been wrongfully deprived of the position. It would have been his had he not been the victim of an injustice. To give it to him, then, is merely to restore to him what is rightfully his. Just as part of the remedy for theft is to restore the stolen property to its rightful owner, the remedy for the injustice done to Jones is to restore to him what would have been his had he not been the victim of an injustice.

We do not think that this argument is self-evident. We do think, however, that it is plausible enough to suggest that there is something wrong with treating the past as though it is morally irrelevant. Doing so does not allow us to think about how to remedy past injustices.

How might we think about the issue from a nonconsequentialist point of view? The starting point must be the idea of respect for persons. What kinds of arrangements can be made that respect the dignity and worth of each of the students in Mrs. Andrews's class?

It is not clear that the idea of respect for persons precludes any trade of the sort we have been discussing. It does seem to limit the extent of the trade, however. Any complete or even extensive trade of the education of one child for the welfare of all would seem to fail to pay proper respect to the unique value of that child. Respect for persons seems to limit the extent to which we can trade one person's welfare for the welfare of all. But what are the limits? What would count as a principled way of deciding what arrangements show respect for the worth of each person?

One answer to this dilemma can be constructed by adapting an idea taken from the contemporary philosopher John Rawls.[1] (Our use of his views takes some liberties.) Rawls has suggested a principle that is intended as an answer to the question of the kinds of inequalities that can be permitted in a just society. His position is that inequality is permissible when it is to the advantage of the least advantaged individual. We must judge inequality from the perspective of the person who is the least well off. Does an existing inequality make that person better

1. John Rawls, *A Theory of Justice* (Cambridge, Mass.: Harvard University Press, 1971).

off or worse off? If an inequality is to the benefit of the person receiving the lesser share, then it is permissible. Otherwise it is not.

Such a principle might be argued for by appealing to the idea of equal respect for persons. How do we decide if we have shown equal respect for the value of each individual? We do so by being able to show that the least well off person in our society is as well off as he or she can be. Any inequalities that exist must be shown to generate benefits for all in which even the least advantaged share.

If we are to apply this view to any proposed arrangements of Mrs. Andrews's reading groups, we will have to look at the effects on the slow readers. If the possibilities are to leave Tim in his current reading group or to put him in the lowest reading group, the question becomes which of these arrangements benefits the slowest readers. If they are better off by having Tim in their group and not disrupting the class, then Tim should be assigned to the lower group. Otherwise some other arrangement must be found.

This view does place limits on the trade. If the effects on Tim are severe, then presumably at some point Tim will become the least advantaged person in the class so far as reading is concerned. If and when this happens, we have reached the limit of the right to trade Tim's progress in reading for the progress of the rest of the class. We cannot make any further trade, even if such a trade would improve the average reading scores of the members of the class. Instead we must consider Tim's welfare. Arguably, such a procedure displays equal respect for the value of each member of the class. Insofar as no person's welfare can be entirely traded for the welfare of the group, all are treated as though they are objects of value. Insofar as the primary concern is to make the least advantaged person as well off as possible, everyone's value is respected equally.

To this point we have assumed that Tim, not Paul, is the one to be misclassified if anyone is going to be. Is that justifiable on nonconsequentialist grounds? Nonconsequentialists, of course, are not going to permit the use of race as a criterion in the decision. Racial discrimination hardly shows respect for persons. Moreover, racial discrimination fails the test of universality. Few of us, we suspect, are likely to will racial discrimination to be a universal rule of human conduct. Few of us will wish to be discriminated against.

This is not altogether decisive, however. It may be that there are contextual factors making it plausible to take race into account in some instances. The most obvious case is that of providing remedies for previous injustice. Here we might argue that while Paul and Tim are equal in their current reading abilities, had it not been for the history of racial discrimination in the United States and its effects on the capacity of the black community to be an educational resource for its own children, Paul would have been ahead of Tim. Thus, Paul should be treated as though he were more advanced than Tim. Nonconsequentialist views permit the past to be morally relevant.

Other contextual factors are also possible. It might be argued that given the history of discrimination against blacks in the United States, a policy that prefers blacks to whites when their qualifications are otherwise equal is not based on any assumption that blacks are somehow inherently entitled to better treatment than whites. Such a policy would not be based on a denial of equal respect. But a policy which preferred whites to blacks would seem to be so based. Racial discrimination is a sufficient part of our past and present that it is reasonable to suspect any policy that results in preferring whites to blacks of being rooted in a denial of equal respect for blacks. Context makes a difference.

This argument can be augmented by suggesting that there are other (consequentialist) reasons for linking some educational decisions to race. We may value the educational consequences of diversity, or we may wish to bring blacks into the mainstream of American life as rapidly as possible. If we can point to some legitimate objective to be achieved by preferential treatment of minorities, and if we can show that the context of our decision is such that it is implausible to hold that our decision is rooted in the belief that whites are less worthy of respect than blacks, then we may be able to reconcile nonconsequentialist values with some forms of preferential treatment.

Mrs. Andrews might argue as follows: "I will move Tim to the lower reading group. I will do this because it will benefit the entire class. While it will not benefit Tim, neither will it so harm him that he will become the slowest reader in the class. Moreover, I will monitor his progress so that if he really does seem in danger of falling behind the rest of the class, I can reconsider the arrangements. I will pick Tim rather than Paul because Paul may have been unfairly disadvantaged by being black, because the harmony and diversity of my class and my reading groups are thereby maintained, and because my decision is not based on the assumption that blacks are inherently entitled to better treatment than whites."

As the reader may have anticipated, this analysis is not problem-free. The nonconsequentialist version of the justification of the trade-off is capable of justifying some implausible trades. What it does do is place a floor under permissible trades. What it does not do is place any limit on how much the group may have to sacrifice to the welfare of the least advantaged member. This may be a particularly difficult question in education. Let us imagine that Mrs. Andrews has a child in her class who is a very slow reader but who nevertheless makes marginal progress if given a great deal of attention by Mrs. Andrews. How much time would Mrs. Andrews be justified in withdrawing from the rest of the class in order to spend it with this one child? If our duty is to maximize the welfare of the least advantaged child, there is virtually no limit on the time Mrs. Andrews should spend with this child. As long as this one child continues to progress and as long as the rest of the class does not fall behind this child, he will have a virtually unlimited claim on Mrs. Andrews's time to the exclusion of the other children. Such an outcome is surely unfair. It requires us to be willing to trade significant achievements of the entire class for the marginal improvement of one child. This cannot be just, but it seems to be required by the principle to which we have been appealing.

The argument for misclassifying Tim instead of Paul is also suspicious. It has one difficulty that is similar to a frequent complaint about benefit maximization. It requires us to know things that seem unknowable. In this case, it is not facts about the future that we are required to know, but facts about the past. If we are to treat Paul as the victim of injustice, it is not enough to know that blacks as a class have been discriminated against. We need to know that Paul has been discriminated against or that he has suffered because of discrimination against other blacks. Do we know this? Are discrimination and its consequences still so pervasive in our society that we can presume that every black is a victim? If not, we will have to be able to show that a given individual was the victim of a particular injustice.

It is also worth noting that in order to make the contextual argument, it has been necessary to abandon the generality of traditional nonconsequentialist positions. We have not asked whether the use of race as a criterion is permissible. We have asked whether the use of race as a deciding criterion is permissible under specified conditions. This can be regarded as an improvement. Here, however, we should ask if we have not made the argument sensitive to context at the price of vagueness. How are we to decide what contextual variables to take into account and what they are to mean for our decisions?

The problem can be reformulated in a more forceful way. It is one thing to know that we are obligated to treat people with equal respect. It is another thing to know what counts as treating people with equal respect. The difficulties we have had in formulating a coherent principle to govern trades between the welfare of individuals and the vagueness of contextual decisions about the use of race as a deciding criterion suggest that achieving a satisfactory understanding of what counts as respect for persons is at best a formidable task.

REFLECTIONS ON METHOD

Let us conclude this discussion with two additional observations concerning moral arguments. First, in this case both consequentialist and nonconsequentialist arguments have been used to construct two very similar results for Mrs. Andrews. Here the moral theory applied seems not to have made very much difference. On the other hand, it would not have been too difficult to argue the other side of the issues using either moral theory. All that would have been needed would have been to alter the facts. Given different assumptions about the facts, one would get different results. This is neither surprising nor problematic. It does, however, serve to remind us of an important feature of moral arguments: They always have both normative and factual premises. When one changes the premises, different conclusions follow. Both kinds of premises are necessary for any recommendation about appropriate action. Moral theories do not supply the facts, but they do tell us how the facts are relevant to moral decisions.

The second point concerns the use of examples in testing our moral intuitions. In the above arguments we have tested the principles suggested to govern the distribution of educational resources by trying to show that in certain kinds of cases they have unacceptable consequences. One might object that some of the cases are implausible. Teachers are not often required, for example, to decide how much time they will give to learners whose learning rates are quite like those described above. Such an objection misses the point of the argument, however. It is not assumed that such decisions are common. What is assumed is that performing thought experiments on extreme cases illuminates the properties and the weaknesses of our moral theories. Ethical theories, like scientific theories, do not have to explain only some of the facts or the most common facts. They have to be able to explain all relevant moral facts and situations. Our moral intuitions about extreme cases are often an important part of moral data. Here, too, as in science, it is often the more esoteric facts that prove illuminating.

Before going on to the next chapter, you may want to consider two additional cases regarding equal treatment of students. One deals with a form of de facto racial segregation, and the other with grading practices where *A*'s in one class would be *C*'s in another.

ADDITIONAL CASES

Equal but Separate

Deerpark School of Sylvan is part of the new Madison County Consolidated School District, a planned realignment of educational facilities and government. The new system combines under a central county administration the old schools of Jefferson City, which have been dominated by minorities and the urban poor in recent years, with the modern schools of the richer suburbs. This plan was developed as a result of pressure from Jefferson City residents and federal attorneys in order to guarantee educational parity and an acceptable racial balance in the area schools. It also provides additional revenue and improved services for the city schools. Under this plan, many students from Jefferson City now attend schools in surrounding towns like Sylvan.

Some teachers have followed these students to their new schools, as part of a limited reassignment of faculty in the new county system. Rosemary Anderson, a fourth-grade instructor, is among this group. Rosemary had come to Jefferson City with the Teachers Corps ten years ago, and she had remained with the city school system afterwards. Her years in these schools had been full of struggle and happiness. She and her fellow teachers had worked hard to provide a decent education for disadvantaged children, using meager resources, determination, and imagination. Rosemary was a bit sad that a period of educational experimentation in Jefferson City had ended, but she believed that the new system would be best for the students in the long run. Her decision to transfer to Deerpark School was based, in part, upon a desire to follow the progress of the Jefferson City children in the new program.

Upon arriving in her new classroom on the first day of school, Rosemary has discovered that she has followed these children much more closely than she had expected. Most of the children in her classroom are from Jefferson City. After consultation with another teacher, Rosemary has found that all of the students in the other fourth-grade class are from the Sylvan area. In her opinion, this state of affairs does not accord with the spirit and intent of the agreement that created the unified county school district. The present arrangement at Deerpark School will only perpetuate de facto racial and economic segregation and minimize the desirable educational objectives that the consolidation plan was designed to encourage. The children in her classroom will have little personal contact with the other students and will remain strangers, possibly antagonists, to the children of Sylvan. Deerpark School seems to have abandoned any official responsibility to direct the racial and cultural interaction that might serve to ameliorate the cleavages that afflict life in Madison County. This will only serve to harm the interests of both groups of children. In a very real sense, the school is an educational failure. It is undemocratic in its practices, and it is not really desegregated. Rosemary Anderson has decided to confront the principal on this matter.

Robert Shire, the principal of Deerpark School and a resident of Sylvan, has attempted to assuage Rosemary's anger and has explained the present placement policy at the school. Deerpark School and the people of Sylvan will comply with the provisions of the consolidation plan, but they also intend to preserve the educational quality of the school. Over the years, Deerpark School has developed a very progressive, unified curriculum and has been very successful in its educational mission. The Jefferson City children will need time to adjust to the new curriculum. Also, the students from the city are not as educationally advanced as their new peers, and the standardized test scores for reading and mathematics show this. It will take time to bring their performances up to the proper grade level. Under these circumstances, Mr. Shire believes that it would be disruptive to instruction and unfair to both groups of children if they are thrown together with no regard for educational attainments. Mr. Shire has asked Rosemary to have patience with the present situation.

Some Questions

1. Is this a case of differences that make a difference? Should the Jefferson City children be treated differently because their reading and math scores are low?
2. Clearly this is a case of legally imposed desegregation that may meet the letter, but not the spirit and purpose, of the new arrangements. Is this a case where what is legal and what is ethical can be meaningfully separate questions? Which should take precedence here?
3. Imagine you are Rosemary. Construct an argument using appropriate ethical principles and ideas that you would present to Mr. Shire and take further, to the board perhaps, if you failed to convince him of your position.
4. We have said that facts enter into ethical reasoning in important ways. Could you alter the facts of this case in a way that justifies the continued de facto segregation of the Jefferson City children?

Grading Policies

David Levine is the chairperson of the social studies department at Henry Hudson High School, a large metropolitan secondary school. Because of the size of the student population, several sections of certain courses are offered each year, and each is taught by a different instructor. In the case of modern American history, three teachers offer courses. Students are assigned to these courses according to a simple alphabetical rotation. This simple system has become a complex problem for Mr. Levine.

The first section is taught by Albert Foley. Mr. Foley is a young, somewhat idealistic teacher who believes that stimulating learning experiences form the core of an education. In his class, he relies upon the study of current events from newspapers and television, and he encourages his students to initiate independent study projects. Mr. Foley is not as much concerned about command of exact facts as he is about the personal significance that modern American history may come to hold for his students. In that direction, he believes, lies the promise of good citizenship. He grades students on the basis of essays about topics they select and journals of personal response to classroom discussion and current events. Among the students, he is known as "Easy *A*" Foley. In a typical year, thirty percent of his students will receive *A*'s, and another thirty percent will receive *B*'s. The rest are given *C*'s, with an occasional *D* for serious cases. Mr. Foley says that a student will pass his class if he is able to find his way to the classroom. In his opinion, it is hard enough being a teenager, and he is not going to make it any tougher. He believes that his children really learn and grow in their sense of self-worth because of his policy.

"The facts and nothing but the facts" might be the motto of William Sampson, the teacher of the second section, for he believes that subject matter is all important. Mr. Sampson relies on the textbook exclusively, and he delivers very detailed lectures. He demands that his students know the facts about American government and recent historical events, and he has very little patience with uninformed opinion. In his view, good citizenship must rest upon a solid foundation of knowledge. He tells his students that they must learn American history backwards and forwards, or they will not pass his course. In order to guarantee this, the students must take rigorous objective examinations that test their knowledge of the most exact matters of fact. In a recent class of forty students, the grades were distributed in the following manner: three *A*'s, five *B*'s, eighteen *C*'s, nine *D*'s, and five *F*'s. Mr. Sampson contends that his tests are fair measures of his students' knowledge. The students call him "Slasher Sampson."

Nancy Wright, the teacher of the third section, believes that life is a competition for finite resources, and her course is taught in a manner that reflects that belief. In the future, her students will have to struggle for pieces of the pie at the table of life. Similarly, in her classroom, they must compete among themselves for places in a hierarchy of achievement, for Ms. Wright grades according to a curve. In her most recent group of forty students there were five *A*'s, ten *B*'s, fifteen *C*'s, seven *D*'s, and three *F*'s, a distribution of grades that she has come to favor after some experience. Ms. Wright uses both essays and objective tests in order to provide some unbiased basis for her judgments. She believes that her proportional approach to grading avoids questions of favoritism and accurately reflects the performance of each student as it compares to that of others in the class. Ms. Wright's students have no nickname for her.

Mr. Levine, the department chairperson, has had many complaints from parents, students, and other teachers about this state of affairs. Each teacher has been criticized on grounds of fairness. According to these critics, the performance of any one student, as measured by the final grade, will vary with the policy of the teacher. It seems that the grades of many students in modern American history depend upon the luck of the draw that originally places them in their respective classes. This is a form of random selection, an attempt to avoid partiality, but is it fair?

Some Questions

1. This case reflects a common educational practice, giving freedom to teachers to structure their own classes and devise their own grading systems. Obviously this can create unequal treatment of students in different sections of the same course or across the same grade level. Should grading procedures be standardized? What would be some arguments for and against standardization?
2. Imagine being each of these teachers in turn—Mr. Foley, Mr. Sampson, and Ms. Wright. How would you defend your approach to grading? How would you respond to Mr. Levine if he told you he thought your approach to teaching American history and your grading system were unfair?
3. Should there be limits on the freedom of teachers to design and carry out their courses in the way they independently judge to be best? On what grounds might such freedom be limited? On what principles might it be defended?

*Immediate escalation
w/ mediation
Unfortunate that bureaucrats
ignore inputs of experienced teachers*

Chapter 5

Democracy, Deliberation, and Reflective Equilibrium

*It is the teacher's moral duty to protect
her children — if she is applauded for
insubordination ... to she
accomplishing this good?*

A CASE TO CONSIDER

Percy Wright, a reporter for the *New World Chronicle*, was investigating a story that had recently broken at New World West Elementary School. The case dealt with Irene Canebrake, a second grade teacher. New World was contemplating taking disciplinary action against Canebrake for refusing to comply with the district's recently approved curriculum guide for mathematics in the elementary schools. The new guide required the introduction of fractions in the second grade. It also specified a testing program for determining the mastery of various mathematical skills, including fractions. Ms. Canebrake, after attempting to teach the required curriculum, had stopped doing so. In her own defense she wrote a note to Angela Dormer, the principal of West Elementary. Her note said that, in her professional judgment, the majority of students in the second grade were not able to deal with fractions. Moreover, the frustration that resulted from being required to master material that was beyond their ability had begun to affect their work in other areas. Her classroom was no longer a happy place. Therefore, she had decided not to teach the curriculum as specified.

Angela Dormer had initially responded by having an informal talk with Ms. Canebrake in which her main message was that Canebrake was free to teach the required curriculum in any way that she saw fit, but that she was not free to ignore it. Ms. Dormer also hinted that blatant insubordination could not be ignored. Canebrake thanked Dormer for her advice, but said that it was a matter of principle with her. The curriculum was harmful to the emotional welfare and educational progress of the children in her charge. Thus she would not teach it. Nor would she engage in the hypocrisy required to pretend to do so in order to satisfy some bureaucratic requirement. If the district felt that it had to take action against her, she was willing to defend her decision before the board. She believed that her duty to her children required this.

Percy Wright had discovered the Canebrake–Dormer conflict because several parents in Irene Canebrake's class had gotten involved. They believed that publicity would be favorable to Canebrake, who had a reputation as an excellent teacher. They had called Wright with their story about how the ''mindless bureaucrats'' in the district were persecuting the best teacher in the school. Percy decided that the case might be of public interest. He interviewed both Irene Canebrake and Angela Dormer and then condensed their remarks. The following is his rendition of their positions. He thought it might make a good article if it was framed as a debate between two personal points of view. His readers would have to decide who was right.

Irene Canebrake: I know that Angela is just trying to do her job, but she has to be able to see this from my point of view. I am responsible for the education and the emotional welfare of these children. I am an experienced teacher. I am well trained in my field. All of my professional knowledge and experience say that this curriculum cannot be taught to these children at this age. I would be irresponsible if I tried to teach it. The children can't learn the material. Trying to teach it to them will generate negative attitudes toward mathematics and will produce unnecessary stress in my classroom. I know some people in the district worked hard on this curriculum guide, but I cannot allow myself to be required to teach in a way that is so obviously harmful to the children in my class. They are my first responsibility. To comply with this curriculum guide when I know that it is harmful to my students would be unethical. Angela should ask herself what she would do in my place. Would she be willing to mistreat these kids because of some silly piece of paper?

Angela Dormer: I understand that Irene is trying to do the best job that she can for her students and that she is conscientiously opposed to the curriculum guide on this matter. However, the curriculum guide was created by a district committee of parents, teachers, and administrators. There was even a sixth-grader there to represent students. They discussed the curriculum for months. They considered the question of whether second grade was too soon for fractions, and, although opinion was divided, they agreed that, in light of the need for higher standards in education, fractions should be introduced early. Even those members of the committee who continued to harbor doubts about the new curriculum eventually were persuaded to lend the policy their provisional support. Whether they are right or wrong, the point is that this curriculum guide has been worked on for a long time by a district committee, and it has been adopted by the school board. Neither Irene nor I are free to substitute our judgment for that of the board of education. Irene should put herself in my place. Am I supposed to overlook the collective judgment of the district curriculum committee and the vote of the school board because Irene believes that they are wrong? Perhaps they are wrong. Nevertheless, I have a duty to enforce district policy.

Having digested the product of his efforts, reporter Wright has decided not to print the story. As he put it to his editor, "If Dormer had been shaking Canebrake down for a few kickbacks or if Canebrake had been molesting her students, our readers might be interested. I could see a good series on ethics in the schools resulting from that. But all these principled disagreements are tedious. I can't see our readers being interested in all this high-mindedness about whether fractions should be taught to second-graders."

Unlike the readers of the *New World Chronicle*, we have the opportunity to consider this case. Once again, the parties disagree in a way that seems unresolvable. How might we respond? Several responses seem possible. On the one hand, one might treat the disagreement as a reason for moral skepticism. The authors of this book, the reader might say, keep on insisting that ethical reasoning has a point and that it is capable of producing results, but they keep on giving us cases that they seem unable to resolve. Why should we believe that ethical reasoning can work? Don't the authors owe us a fuller account of how ethical reasoning should work to resolve such issues? On the other hand, one might treat this case as demonstrating the need for an inquiry into legitimate authority. When two parties in a dispute disagree and when some decision must be made, how do we decide who is entitled to decide? Who has the right to make the final decision? Finally, the case raises questions about the nature of the ethical deliberative process itself. One might argue that what this case calls for is more dialogue between the contesting parties. They need to talk the matter out more and come to some consensus. Maybe they stopped talking too soon. Maybe an understanding of the conditions of productive ethical dialogue needs to be spelled out.

In what follows, we will address these three concerns. First, we will characterize what we call *reflective equilibrium*. This will provide a fuller description of ethical reasoning. Second, we will discuss the problem of sovereignty or authority. In schools, especially public schools, when people disagree, who is entitled to make the decision? Where does sovereignty come from? How is it justified? Finally, we want to discuss ethical deliberation as a social process. Here we want to insist that a social process of ethical dialogue is not just nice, but necessary. Moral deliberation is inherently a social process and, as such, has some special features that are important to validating ethical decisions. We turn first to a fuller description of our view of ethical reasoning.

REFLECTIVE EQUILIBRIUM

Dumb statement

The reader should not be overly distressed by the many instances of moral ambiguity we have presented in this book. Ethical matters are not always so contestable. Nevertheless, the fact is that people disagree. Even when they disagree deeply and for a very long time, however, it does not mean that reasoned agreement in ethics is forever impossible. In the sciences, for example, matters that were topics of disagreement for a long time seem to get resolved eventually. Thus the existence of persistent disagreement may be taken as a reason for believing that even though a matter is difficult, it need not be unresolvable. Even in ethics, some issues about which people have long disagreed have eventually come to be resolved. For example, human beings were unclear about the morality of slavery for centuries. Yet today the immorality of slavery can be taken as an established moral principle. We also need to be careful to avoid inappropriate expectations of ethical reasoning. Ethics is more like law than math or science in its degree of precision and its aspirations. While ethics, like law, can be studied and used to deal with real problems, it is not capable of the same degree of conclusiveness as mathematics; and its purpose is not to achieve a description of the world as it is, but of how it ought to be. We see the purpose of ethical deliberation as seeking to achieve agreement on principles that regulate human action while respecting the equal worth and the interests of all. We suggest that reflective equilibrium is the appropriate standard for such an activity and that extensive dialogue is a requirement for its achievement.

We will begin our account of reflective equilibrium with a brief sketch of our position. The central ideas are these: Moral decisions regarding choice and action require moral sensitivity, rationality, and the development of moral theory for which the primary evidence is our moral intuitions. Moral intuitions, our sense of what is right and wrong, are the basic data for moral reasoning and the construction of moral theory.

Not every moral intuition is equally useful, however. We should begin with those which seem compelling and uncontroversial. Constructing a moral theory then proceeds through attempts to formulate principles that account for these moral intuitions. We must be able to describe the underlying moral concepts that generate our sense of right and wrong, to discover the implicit rules that cause us to feel the way we do. It is not just taking whatever pops into our hearts and heads as right or wrong; it is looking for the bases of our intuitions, describing and analyzing them, and then testing them to the best of our ability.

In this respect, constructing a moral theory is much like attempting to describe the rules governing our sense of grammar. We have intuitions about how to use language correctly and meaningfully without necessarily being able to formulate the rules of our language. This sense of what is meaningful or correct to say provides the data against which to test sets of rules postulated in order to explain our sense of grammar. In fact, that is how grammarians do grammar. They will ask themselves questions such as "Why does 'All good boys eat cake' make sense and 'Cake boys good eat all' not make sense?" Likewise, we must make clear and explicit the rules and principles that underlie our moral intuitions.

The analogy goes even deeper. Sometimes a deep understanding of the principles of language can lead us to revise our initial opinion about what is meaningful or correct. Understanding the principle can make an expression that seemed obscure or ambiguous clear and comprehensible, or it can lead us to see the awkwardness or obscurity of something that had appeared clear and simple. Likewise, a moral theory can change or overrule our intuitions about moral phenomena. Once we see more clearly what is assumed by our moral intuitions, we may wish to change them. Thus, there is an interaction between moral theory and moral intuition in ethical reflection, each influencing the other. The trick is to achieve some point of reflective equilibrium between our moral sense and our moral theory. By reflective equilibrium we mean reaching a point in our deliberations where we feel that our moral intuitions and the moral theory that accounts for them are satisfactorily consistent and where the decisions we reach and actions we take can be justified by our moral theory. Of course, as with scientific theory, new facts, events, and hypotheses can force us to reconsider and reformulate our moral theory and to alter our decisions and actions.

Moral theories must meet the standards common to judging theories of all sorts. They must explain the data appropriate to them. They must be consistent. Elegance, parsimony, and symmetry are nice, too, when they can be had. Moral theories must also be sensitive to knowledge in other domains. Factual matters and the theories of other disciplines are important to ethical theory, not only because they are important in knowing how moral abstractions are applied to concrete cases, but also because they can suggest new problems to be solved or alter the concepts by means of which ethical theories are articulated. Freud's discovery of the unconscious raised difficult questions for the notion of autonomy and posed new moral issues about psychological manipulation. The advances of physics and biology drove purposes from nature and required people to rethink the way in which values and purposes exist. These are things that any comprehensive moral theory must confront.

Having a comprehensive and well thought out moral theory is not enough. As feeling human beings we also need to be sensitive to the moral domain and draw upon our shared ability to empathize with and care about other persons. Our moral intuitions are rooted in our ability to feel and empathize as well as in our ability to think. We need both emotion and reason to be moved to act morally as well as to care about rational moral arguments and their outcomes. Feelings interact with moral reasoning in several important ways. First, feelings help us to put ourselves in the place of others, to identify with them, to know what hurts and what helps. It will do little good to be committed to respecting the value and dignity of other persons if we cannot experience life from their point of view. How else shall we know how to respect them? How else shall we discover what counts as affirming their dignity?

Second, feelings provide motivation for right conduct. If one could build a computer capable of engaging in moral reasoning, its chief defect would probably be that it would not care about being moral. Knowing what is right and wanting to do it are different things. Our ability to empathize, to experience the wrong done to others as our hurt and the good done to others as our joy, is a large part of our desire to do right. Immanuel Kant, who had many wise things to say about ethics, said nothing wiser than that the only really good thing is a good will.

How, then, do we settle ethical arguments? We proceed first by trying to discover the moral principles that underlie our differing senses of right and wrong. When we see what it is that our moral intuitions assume, perhaps some will change their minds. If not, then we must test our conflicting moral principles by seeing what else follows from them. If we find that some proposed principle leads to an abhorrent result in certain cases, that is a reason to abandon it. Perhaps some will change their minds when they see what else they must agree to if they are to hold consistently to their current principles.

We must now ask, where do our ethical intuitions come from? This question would seem to bear on how far it is possible to establish any reflective equilibrium about ethical issues that is objective. Some philosophers have argued that our sense of morality is innate. Others have suggested that moral intuitions are a kind of seeing. There are moral facts that we can see with our mind's eye, just as we see colors with our physical eye. Others assume that we learn our moral principles, just as we learn our native language, from our culture. Does it matter? One might argue that if moral concepts are innate or involve seeing moral facts that have objective existence, then that certifies the objectivity of moral thought. Moral questions, like questions about the physical world, have answers. On the other hand, if we acquire those principles that generate our moral intuitions from our culture, that means that, fundamentally, relativism is still true. The best that moral reasoning could be expected to do in that case would be to produce a higher level of agreement among those who already agree about basic assumptions.

We believe, however, that the question of where our moral intuitions come from is not that decisive. Seeing it as decisive rests on inflated demands for what will be permitted to count as objective knowledge and an excessive pessimism about human commonalities. If we demand certainty of moral knowledge or if we demand that all legitimate knowledge somehow inheres in the ultimate nature of existence, we may find knowledge difficult to come by—and not only about ethics. If we insist only on establishing a provisional reflective equilibrium, we will have set a standard for objectivity that can often be met and will serve us well in our lives. What is the point of setting our standards for objective knowledge in a way that makes a fundamental and necessary human activity, that of reflecting on what we ought to do, appear impossible?

Moreover, even if our ethical intuitions are acquired from our society, it does not follow that reflective equilibrium between members of different societies is impossible. To the degree that societies are different, we may expect the search for reflective moral equilibrium to be difficult. To assume that it is impossible is to neglect the extent to which all societies are composed of people with a common biology, common fundamental needs, a common physical environment, and common aspirations. It is also to neglect the extent to which we live on a planet whose people are increasingly united by a common science and by common global problems. These commonalities are basic to our view of the source of the moral intuitions of human beings. We are not all so alike that reflective equilibrium about moral matters is likely to be easy. We are not all so different that it must be impossible. Some of us would even argue that we see in human history writ large a positive development of a more humane and more broadly shared ethical point of view. There are, then, some good reasons to keep open the possibility of humanly arrived at ethical knowledge. We can be rational and objective without being certain, and we can be tolerant and open to other points of view without being relativists.

Nevertheless, there is a common but misguided incentive for the prevalent modern belief in moral relativism. It is the human desire to be free, to be unencumbered by duties and obligations. If we may misparaphrase Dostoevski, people seem to believe that if relativism is true, then everything is permitted. Each of us may do as we choose, and no one can tell us that we are wrong or that we must do something else. The idea is often captured in the suggestion that people who argue that something is genuinely right or wrong are in reality attempting to impose their views on others.

This response is both confused and problematic. It is confused in that it identifies compulsion with persuasion. When one person attempts to give reasons to another person, that act is not an attempt at coercion. Indeed, persuasion is a form of influence that recognizes individuals as free moral agents with rational minds and human feelings. To attempt to persuade someone is to assume that the choice is theirs and that as responsible moral agents they would wish to make it on the basis of the best reasons available. To give people reasons is to confirm their status as free people who have the right to choose for themselves.

Seeing persuasion as a kind of coercion ultimately rests on a failure to understand the ultimate moral basis of freedom. We are not free because we have no objective duties. Nothing about freedom follows from moral relativism, because nothing at all concerning ethical matters can follow from relativism. We are free because we are moral agents with the duty to decide for ourselves and because it is morally offensive to interfere arbitrarily with the liberty of a person who has the moral duty to make responsible choices.

It is often claimed that what sets human beings off from other living creatures is their ability to reason. From our point of view, we humans also share the distinctive capacity to have and choose to have obligations. To ask what moral obligations we should accept is to presume that we are free to choose and that good reasons can be given for some choices and against others. And the giving of reasons presumes that reasons provide objective grounds for reaching potential agreements and progressive states of reflective equilibrium and moral growth.

Relativism is problematic in that, if taken seriously, it can lead us to withhold resources that are important for moral growth. People do not learn to make responsible choices by being told that it does not matter what they decide, since one choice is as good as another. They learn to make responsible choices by learning to appraise arguments and consider evidence relevant to what they have to decide. Such things are best learned by participating in a milieu in which ethical matters are seriously considered and debated. Moral relativism undermines the moral education appropriate to a free people.

THE QUESTION OF SOVEREIGNTY

Perhaps, then, in the long run, after much debate and deliberation, ethical agreement is possible. However, sometimes decisions need to be made in the short run even though people continue to disagree. Then we need to know what legitimates a decision under conditions of disagreement. What confers sovereignty (that is, the authority or right to decide)?

Consider a simple-minded position. Let us suppose that what gives a person the right to decide some matter is that the person knows what the best thing to do is. This might be the position of Irene Canebrake. She feels entitled to refuse to teach the new math curriculum simply because she *knows* that it is not in the children's best interest. However, this is not a tenable position, since in cases of conflict it is, by definition, unclear who is right. Thus it is unhelpful to claim that the person who should decide is the person who is right. We need to keep separate the question of what the right decision is from the question of what constitutes legitimacy in decision making. Both are important, of course, but we must be able to decide whether a decision is legitimate even when (especially when!) we disagree about which decision is best. How can we do this?

One response is that legitimate decisions are those achieved by a legitimate process. We might, for example, hold that decisions are legitimated by voting and that a particular decision is confirmed when it achieves a majority of votes. Such a view tells us how decisions are legitimated, and it locates sovereignty in the majority, but nothing guarantees that the decisions of a majority are the best ones.

Fortunately, there are other candidates for legitimating procedures that also speak to the question of making the right decision. Let us return to Irene Canebrake's view and see if we can describe it in a less simple-minded fashion. We might claim that the right to make decisions should be given to those who are in the best position to know what is right. On this interpretation, Irene would be claiming sovereignty over the decision, not because she is right, but because she is in the best position of all concerned parties to know what decision is best for her children. She is the trained and experienced teacher, and she best knows the children in her class. Thus she should be given the right to decide. We shall call this position, in which legitimacy is conferred by reason of expertise, *professionalism.*

Professionalism maintains that authority should be vested in those who are most capable of making the best decision. Of course, in our day, advocates of professional decision making also recognize the legitimacy of democratic processes. However, they often wish to argue that, even in a democratic society, some decisions (for example, how to conduct brain surgery) should be made not by majority vote, but by those who have special competence. Thus arguments for professionalism are arguments about when democratic authority is inappropriate or ineffective and when the power to decide is best vested in an expert individual or professional group.

One purpose of democratic decision making is to make sure that everyone's interest in a decision is fairly considered. However, when individuals or special groups gain unencumbered power to make decisions about public matters, they may make these decisions in ways that are most attentive to their own welfare. As Lord Acton noted, power tends to corrupt. Democracy addresses this problem by giving everyone equal power over public decisions and a voice in public deliberations. In representative democracies these things are accomplished (imperfectly) by elections and by such rights as free speech and a free press and freedom of petition and assembly. Elected officials represent the people and must undergo scrutiny and criticism. When the people disapprove of how they are represented, they may vote the rascals out.

Nevertheless, there may be cases in which democracy is especially ineffective in protecting the public interest. Some decisions may require "esoteric knowledge." Esoteric knowledge is knowledge that is not available to the ordinary person, usually because it is the product of lengthy training. When decisions require esoteric knowledge to be made competently, democratic institutions may be ineffective means for making these decisions because the citizenry or their elected representatives may lack the competence to evaluate the decisions adequately. In such cases, it may be desirable to vest those who possess the required knowledge, the experts, with authority.

Often professional authority is exercised by a professional organization that is explicitly empowered to make certain decisions by a democratic body such as a state legislature. Such organizations are given three interconnected powers. First, they are given the authority to legitimate a knowledge base. They engage in a variety of deliberative processes that result in the identification of what is to count as professional knowledge and how it is to be assessed. Second, they govern the professional practice of their members. They do this by prescribing what counts as competent practice and by disciplining members who practice incompetently or unethically. Finally, professions control the initiation of new members into the profession. They do this both by prescribing and conducting their education and by determining the qualifications for licensure.

When authority over decisions is transferred to professionals, how are we to be sure that it is exercised in the interest of the people? The usual response to this question is that professionals are taught an ethic that emphasizes maintaining professional standards and client welfare. Thus it is the training of professionals, their initiation into an ethic of professional responsibility and service, that primarily serves to ensure that professionals serve the public.

Irene Canebrake's argument makes the most sense if one sees it as an expression of professionalism in education. She has appealed to her training and experience, her expertise, to legitimate her authority over the math curriculum in her class. She has claimed that she should make the decision because she is in a position to make the best decision. She has also made a strong appeal to an ethic of professionalism. She has claimed that her first duties are to her profession and its standards of good practice and to the welfare of the children in her classroom. These duties outweigh her responsibilities to her administrative superiors and to the school board.

Does this argument succeed? In one respect it is clear that it does not. It is currently the case that the law locates sovereignty over education not in teachers or their organizations, but in state legislatures and in school boards, both of which are elected legislative bodies. Such bodies may choose to respect the decisions of the teachers they employ, but they are not obliged to do so. Legally, teaching is not currently structured as a profession.

Perhaps this is unwise. The public interest in education might be better served if teaching was recognized as a profession and if teachers had more autonomy in their work. This is an issue that is currently being hotly debated. Moreover, it is a complex issue that cannot be decided here. But we do wish to make a few observations about it.

In our society arguments in favor of professionalizing teaching are often arguments against the democratic governance of education. If teachers are to govern their own practice, then the right of state legislatures or local school boards to make an extensive range of educational decisions will have to be diminished or restricted. A new division of labor between elected authorities and professional teachers will have to be forged. Sovereignty over education will be relocated. That professionalism is competitive with democracy in this way does not mean that it is undesirable or incompatible. But it does mean that a case must be made that is adequate to rebut a presumption in favor of democratic authority. This is true even when expert knowledge is required in decision making.

Such a case requires two things. First, there must be an adequate knowledge base to ground a profession of teaching. The crucial feature of Irene Canebrake's case for authority over the conduct of her classroom is that she, and not others, is in a position to know what is best for her students. If such claims are a basis for professionalism, then teachers must possess expert knowledge that is genuinely esoteric. Teachers must be like doctors in that their education renders them uniquely capable of making competent professional choices. Second, the education teachers receive must be sufficient to establish an ethic of professional responsibility and client welfare. It is such an ethic that ensures that professional autonomy serves the public interest.

Angela Dormer's case against Irene Canebrake is an argument for democratic authority. Angela regards herself as entitled to enforce the school district's curriculum policy because that policy was democratically arrived at and because she has been appointed by the duly constituted democratic authority to administer its decisions. The curriculum policy was developed by a suitably representative committee consisting of parents, teachers, and administrators. It was adopted by the school board. Angela does not argue that this process is the one that is most likely to make the best decision. Instead she seems to claim that the decision is legitimate because it was democratically achieved.

Angela regards her own authority as deriving from the authority of the board of education. She was hired by them to implement their decisions. Consequently, she is bound by board policy. She sees Irene as similarly obligated. In accepting employment by the New World School District, Irene has become a public servant bound by the authority of democratically elected officials. To assert her judgment against theirs is to reject the legitimacy of democratic authority.

If we look closely we will see that Angela's arguments appeal to two different visions of what democracy is about. Initially, Angela appeals to the fact that the curriculum policy was created by a committee that represented various interests in the school, that the committee engaged in extensive deliberations, and that eventually all members of the committee agreed. Later, however, Angela appeals to the fact that the committee's policy was adopted by the school board as her central argument. She seems to regard the school board as the final authority and sees her own authority as deriving from the board's.

The two visions of democracy expressed in these two different arguments can be distinguished from each other. In the first argument, Angela appeals to what we call *communitarian democracy*. It has three central features. First, it takes the participants in the democratic process to be those individuals who are currently within the school community. Second, it emphasizes the importance of discussion and rational deliberation in decision making. Third, it seeks consensus and tries to avoid circumstances in which majorities enforce their will on minorities.

This view of democracy seems committed to the idea that decisions are legitimated when they are the product of uncoerced discussion and consensus among community members. The community here is not the larger community of citizens who live within the boundaries of the school district. It consists of those who are, in one way or another, directly involved in the school. Moreover, it tends to see deliberation and consensus as more important than voting in legitimating decisions.

Angela emphasizes that the district's policy is legitimated because it was achieved by such a process. The appeal of the argument to Irene Canebrake is best described as an appeal to her sense of identification with the school community. Angela is saying to Irene: "Look, this is what we decided. In resisting the decision, you are withdrawing from the community. You seem no longer to be one of us." The view that affiliation is cemented by open participation and that resisting the consensus once achieved ruptures the community is a significant part of the ethos of any democratic community and a powerful means of legitimating decisions.

This view of democracy does not provide an adequate account of sovereignty in public schools. Public schools are financed by taxes, which are collected, directly or indirectly, from state and local citizens. Moreover, these citizens have interests in the quality and character of education even when they do not directly participate in the affairs of the school. Thus the curriculum committee, as constituted in this case, does not represent the interests of taxpayers or other citizens. If sovereignty over educational decisions were to reside in such internal committees and if educational decisions could be made by participants in the school in a way that was unchecked by the larger community, then several important tenets of democracy would be violated. There would be taxation without representation. Citizens of the community would find themselves unable to influence schools even though they were taxed to pay for them, were required to send their children to them, and underwent the consequences of the success or failure of the education provided. These are all reasons to hold that sovereignty must reside outside the immediate school community and should be vested in the elected representatives of the citizenry. Let us call this form of democracy *representative democracy*.

An appeal to representative democracy is Angela Dormer's trump card in her disagreement with Irene Canebrake. In a democratic society sovereignty over public education ultimately rests in elected legislative bodies. To oppose the authority of the school board is to oppose representative democracy.

In our society, given its political traditions, it is hard not to agree that ultimately Angela Dormer is right. At the same time, we should note the dark side of representative democracy. School districts are typically large entities. Their boundaries may include thousands or even millions of citizens. They may employ hundreds or even thousands of teachers and administrators, and they may teach many thousands of students. Given such large organizations, it is unlikely that school board members will be able to participate directly in the affairs of any given school. Instead, school boards will make policy and hire administrators to implement it. Teachers will be employees who owe a duty to their employer. They may or may not exercise independent judgment as their employer decides, but to resist the will of their employer once expressed is to commit the sin of insubordination against democratic authority. Such schools are likely to be hierarchically organized. Teachers will be the lowest link in a chain of command. Locating sovereignty in a remote legislative body can make teachers into people who merely implement decisions made elsewhere, by individuals whose competence in matters of education is far from assured. This may deny teachers a voice in policy and may deny schools the benefit of their wisdom and their involvement in decision making. In some cases it may force on them a choice between their professional ethic and their duty to their employer. Even if Irene Canebrake's professionalism argument is insufficient to entitle her to sovereignty over what goes on in her classroom, we should not ignore the fact that she may indeed be the person who is in the best position to know what is best for her children.

These observations suggest two conclusions. One is that in considering how decisions are to be made in schools there are different views of how to locate authority that serve different values. Professionalism emphasizes expertise and competence, communitarian democracy emphasizes participation and discussion, and representative democracy emphasizes equal representation of the citizenry. All of these values seem commendable. At the same time, it seems difficult to serve them all simultaneously. A second conclusion is that, whenever disagreement is so deep that we must raise the issue of sovereignty, in our society we must conclude that sovereignty rests in the people unless the people vest it elsewhere. This means that teachers, who are not legally professionals, will have to respect the decisions of legislatures even if they regard them as wrong. (Of course, this does not mean that there are no legal or morally right ways to contest bad decisions. Nor does it mean that teachers are not entitled to pursue professional status for themselves.)

At the same time it is important to see that much is lost when issues can be resolved only by asserting sovereignty. In what follows we suggest that some of what is lost can be recovered if we are more attentive to the character of ethical dialogue and more concerned with dialogue than with sovereignty. We shall address two questions: (1) What makes ethical dialogue important? and (2) What are the features of a good dialogue?

ETHICAL DIALOGUE

One might argue that Irene Canebrake was at fault for not trying harder to present her case to the school community. We might say, "She should have gone to the curriculum committee and tried to explain what had happened in her class" or "She was too confrontational; she did not give Angela Dormer and the school board a chance to reconsider." These observations see the problem as requiring more dialogue, not as requiring the location of sovereignty. The issue should be talked out. Why?

Consider two kinds of values that dialogue might serve. We will call these *values of community* and *values of rationality*.[1]

Dialogue often strengthens community. It can reinforce a sense of common enterprise and thereby create a sense of membership. Through dialogue *the* school can be transformed into *my* school, *its* goals into *my* goals, *its* activities into *my* activities. When decisions are achieved through dialogue, individuals who participate are more likely to own decisions and to care conscientiously for their implementation. Even when dialogue fails to achieve agreement, it may foster respect and understanding. People may be able to see the issue from the perspective of the other person and to tolerate differences when consensus is beyond reach. All of these features seem important to an organization if it

---

1. Much of the position we develop in this section has been inspired by the work of Jürgen Habermas on the ideal speech community and by John Dewey's insistence on the importance of community in democracy and education.

is to accomplish its tasks in a purposeful and conscientious manner. They are also important features of an organization in which work is rewarding and personal relations are satisfying.

In contrast, the frequent exercise of sovereignty can degrade community. When people are motivated only by a sense of duty to obey some authority, or worse, when they feel coerced by authority, they will not do their work out of loyalty to the community, its purposes, or its members. When community is broken, people are less likely to do their jobs well. Often, when educators resist treating disagreements as occasions for the exercise of sovereignty and instead seek more dialogue, they are seeking to preserve community. Dialogue also serves reasoned inquiry. It provides people with an opportunity to learn from others. They can acquire new concepts and new ways of understanding. Ideas can be subjected to criticism. Those who have special expertise can have the opportunity to share it. This social process of reflection is especially important for ethical issues. We have represented moral reflection as an attempt to express ethical intuitions in principles and to extend these principles to and test them against additional cases. We also insist that ethical reflection should be seen as a social process. There are several reasons for this. First, any process of reflection is improved when insights are shared. Second, the ethical principles that operate in a social institution must be public. They should be known and shared. This is unlikely to be the case unless they are publicly discussed and debated. Finally, dialogue about ethical issues and concepts provides the context in which the sophistication of individuals about ethical issues can be developed. We do not believe that what you have learned from this book can have an enduring effect unless the concepts that it has taught are reinforced and deepened by further conversations about ethics. Teachers are not likely to master these concepts unless they become part of conversations with fellow teachers in schools. Ethical concepts are social creations and social resources. Their vitality and sophistication are sustained by dialogue. Reflective equilibrium is as much a social affair as an individual one.

There may be an additional reason why dialogue is crucial in ethical reflection. Some ethical decisions may be validated by virtue of the fact that those who are involved agree to them. On first reflection this may seem problematic. Obviously agreement is not always a guarantee of truth. The world would not be flat even if everyone agreed that it was. Or imagine that a group of criminals agreed that it would be okay for them to rob a bank and murder all the witnesses. It does not seem reasonable to suggest that their agreement makes their robbery and murder okay.

However, the suggestion that the rightness of ethical decisions or principles is validated by agreement can be made more plausible by noting two things. First, when we engage in a process of dialogue and investigation about some such assertion as "the world is round," it seems plausible to suppose that what we are trying to do is to find out the shape of the world. The statement "the world is round" is true if, in fact, that is how the earth is shaped. But when you are reflecting about ethical issues, it is less clear that we are trying to achieve a description of reality and that our claim is true only if reality is actually that way. If ethical claims are not attempts to describe an independent reality, but rather are claims about what we should take to be fair, just, and right, then agreement among involved parties may play a different role in judging the adequacy of ethical principles and decisions.

Second, we may need to examine the nature of the agreement in our example of murder and robbery more closely. The victims of the murder and robbery were not party to the agreement. Might they have been? Can we imagine a dialogue between the robbers and their intended victims that would lead the latter to agree to being robbed and murdered? Perhaps we might. But the dialogue would be likely to have some unusual characteristics. Perhaps the victims would be coerced. They would agree because they were threatened in some way. Or perhaps they would be deceived about what they were agreeing to.

Thus not any agreement is sufficient to legitimate an ethical decision or choice. Instead, the agreement must be a consensus resulting from a dialogue that meets certain conditions. For example, the participants cannot have been coerced or deceived. Perhaps, then, any ethical decision that can validate an ethical choice must be the result of a dialogue that meets the following conditions: All of the relevant parties must be included in the discussion. The discussion must be "undominated," that is, no one should be coerced, indoctrinated, or manipulated, and everyone should be on an equal footing. No one should play a role in the discussion that can only be explained as a consequence of the exercise of power over others. The decision should be fully aired, with no relevant considerations repressed and no arguments excluded. Finally, a decision reached by such a conversation should satisfy a condition that we will call *reciprocity*. Individual participants in the decision should be able and willing to project themselves into the perspective of other parties in the discussion and to find any decision reasonable from the variety of available perspectives, not only from their own. These conditions define an *open and undominated dialogue*.

These considerations place the question of agreement in a different light. It does seem possible to think that ethical decisions are legitimated, at least in part, because they express a consensus reached by such a dialogue. That an ethical decision results from an open and undominated discussion may be a factor that actually contributes to its being a right decision. One reason for believing this is that the kind of dialogue we have been describing satisfies the principle of respect for persons. It creates conditions in which people are treated as equals. All interests are respected. Everyone's view is taken into account. People are treated as ends, not means. Thus we might view open, undominated dialogue as the principle of equal respect for persons applied to the social process of ethical deliberation.

Perhaps, then, we should resist having to choose between professionalism and democracy and instead insist on more open and undominated discussion. We have identified at least four important values that are served by open, undominated dialogue. Such dialogue helps build community; it facilitates reasoning; and it helps initiate people into the concepts and processes required for sophisticated ethical deliberation. Finally, the fact that an ethical decision emerges from an open and undominated dialogue may itself be a factor that makes the decision morally right.

This discussion has also helped us identify some of the features that make an ethical dialogue a good dialogue. We think that these features are effectively summarized by the phrase *open, undominated dialogue.* Open dialogue accepts input from all relevant participants. Moreover, it respects evidence and argument and thus does not attempt to exclude any relevant consideration from expression. Undominated dialogue avoids infecting discussion with unequal power relations. It insists that discussions respect the equal worth and the equality of interests of participants.

These ideas suggest that discussion is essential to ethical deliberation. Ethical deliberation should be thought of as a social activity conducted cooperatively. The reflective equilibrium that is sought in ethical dialogue is a social outcome. Persistent disagreement indicates that reflective equilibrium has not been achieved.

That ethical deliberation should be seen as a social and dialogical activity leads to two observations about the ethical lives of teachers in schools. We shall conclude this discussion with them. First, the character of schools in our society typically makes the ethical reflection that teachers engage in a solitary affair. Teachers work in self-contained classrooms. There are few forums in schools where it is natural to discuss ethical issues. Moreover, many schools are hierarchically structured in ways that interfere with any real dialogical process. As a consequence, teachers are unlikely to have much opportunity to engage in open and undominated ethical dialogue. If we are right about this, it is a significant shortcoming of our school systems.

Second, teachers need to be careful in how they think about their own integrity in ethical decision making. If one thinks of ethical deliberation as something one does alone, one may also think of the resulting choices in an uncompromising way. One may reason: "I achieved this decision as the result of the best moral reflection of which I am capable. It expresses my best judgment about what is right. Since I believe this choice to be the right thing to do, I am obligated to pursue it, regardless of what others may think. I cannot compromise my principles. My integrity is at stake." People who draw this conclusion run the risk of irreconcilable conflict with others who may have reflected with equal conscientiousness but reached different conclusions. Both Angela Dormer and Irene Canebrake appear to have done this. Both have taken a position from which they cannot move without sacrificing their integrity.

Sometimes ethical people have to resist compromising their integrity. However, if we recognize that ethical reflection is a social and dialogical process as well as an individual one and that one factor in the rightness of a decision is the ability to persuade others of it as the result of an undominated dialogue, we will be less likely to experience a threat to our integrity every time we find that we are in disagreement with someone else about the ethical thing to do. We will be more likely to go the extra mile in seeking consensus before we dig ourselves into a moral foxhole. Finally, we will be less likely to initiate a decision process in which the decision turns more on the question of who has sovereignty than on an open, undominated deliberative process that serves community.

CONCLUSIONS

Much of our analysis of the cases in this book was done by contrasting consequentialist and nonconsequentialist views. (This is one way, but certainly not the only way, to structure discussion about ethical dilemmas.) Is there any reason to prefer one of these orientations to the other? We have only a few brief suggestions to make. The first is that neither view is sufficient. The second is that each view to some extent makes up for the deficiencies of the other. Perhaps we should ask if they can be combined.

In our view, nonconsequentialist concepts are more fundamental. One reason for this is that they are often presupposed by consequentialist views. To see why, let us ask the following question of utilitarianism. When we are calculating the average happiness of individuals, why should we count everyone's happiness as equivalent? Perhaps some people are inherently more worthwhile than others and, thus, their happiness should count more. In calculating the average utility we should multiply the happiness of individuals by a factor reflecting their intrinsic worth. To explain why this suggestion is offensive, we will quickly be led to nonconsequentialist concepts such as equal respect for persons, impartiality, and universality.

The chief difficulty with nonconsequentialist views is that they cannot be coherently applied without a knowledge of what is good for human beings and of how actions affect the welfare of others. Perhaps the average utility principle does not capture well the idea of respect for persons. If that is true, then the conclusion to draw is that we need other principles that show us how to decide what kinds of consequences do capture the idea of equal respect. A viable ethical theory will embed a concern for consequences within a framework of nonconsequentialist ideals.

We conclude with a comment on a consideration that has been a substantial motivating factor behind the approach of this book. We have spent a good deal of time discussing ethical relativism and contrasting consequentialist and nonconsequentialist views. We have done this because we believe that understanding them makes a difference not only in how teachers ought to behave toward students, but in our basic understanding of what education is about.

Socrates is recorded as saying that the unexamined life is not worth living. Why not? In our view, the point of this maxim is that to fail to reflect on how one lives is to fail to recognize one's status as a moral agent. It is to refuse to accept responsibility for one's self. In a fundamental way, it is to refuse to be a person.

We have been unhappy with utilitarianism because it is happiness, not growth as persons, that is the first concern for utilitarians. Growth must be a contingent value and subservient to happiness. We have been unhappy with relativism because it destroys the point of moral growth, as it destroys the point of everything.

In our view, the compelling matter is growth as a moral agent, as someone who cares about others and is willing and able to accept responsibility for one's self, as someone who can engage in open, undominated dialogue with others about a common life and accept shared responsibility for the group's life. Promoting this kind of development is what teachers ought to be fundamentally about, whatever else it is that they are about. We are first and foremost in the business of creating persons. It is our first duty to respect the dignity and value of our students and to help them to achieve their status as free, rational, and feeling moral agents.

It has been traditional to inscribe profound maxims over the entrances of schools. Our suggestion for what ought to be there is contributed by Dr. Seuss. "A person's a person no matter how small."

POST SCRIPT

Professors Strike and Soltis have gone to lunch with several students and a colleague from the philosophy department. The students have just finished *The Ethics of Teaching*. Both the philosopher and the students seem bothered by the book. The following conversation results.

Student 1: When I went home on break, I took your book with me, and my father looked through it. He is quite unhappy with it. He says that ethics cannot be discussed apart from religion and that he suspects you two of being secular humanists. I don't want to go that far, but it does seem to me that my religious training is a part of my ethical outlook. I have a hard time thinking about ethics apart from it.

Student 2: It never occurred to me to think of you guys as secular humanists. But it does seem to me that you've left a lot out. I've been reading a couple of feminist authors. They talk a lot about caring, and they have argued that the kind of ethics you guys write about is male ethics. Shouldn't the ethics of education have something to say about teachers caring about students?

Philosopher: Not only have you two ignored religion and caring— you've ignored most of the history of philosophy! You write as if the only philosophers who have ever existed are Kant and a few utilitarians. How about Aristotle or Plato or Dewey? They've all had some rather profound things to say about both ethics and education. How come no mention of them?

Strike: (looking distinctly uncomfortable) Um . . . ah . . . Well at least I'm fairly sure I'm not a secular humanist. Actually I'm a Presbyterian. But I do have to admit that the view of ethics we present is quite secular and that Kant and utilitarianism figure centrally in the text. However, this text is written for use by prospective teachers who may hold various religious beliefs or none, and who will have to teach in public schools. There are some obvious problems in trying to teach ethics from a religious position if the ethics is for public institutions. If ethics can't be separated from religion in some way, it's hard to see how we could talk about ethics in public contexts without violating someone's freedom of religion.

Soltis: (looking his usual confident self) Perhaps Plato might help us understand why ethics must be independent of religion. Plato wrote a dialogue entitled *Euthyphro* in which he discusses the nature of piety. I can suggest an argument that is not quite Plato's but has much in common with it. Suppose someone said that right actions are those actions commanded or willed by God. A modern Socrates (Plato's voice in his dialogues) might ask how it is that God always commands that which is right. There are two answers, neither of which is very satisfactory. One is that right is whatever it is that God commands us to do and wrong is whatever God forbids. But if that were true, God might command murder and that would make murder right, or He might forbid kindness and that would make kindness evil.

Student 1: But I never believed that God just went around arbitrarily commanding and forbidding things. I always assumed that He was righteous and good, and therefore He would only command things that were themselves righteous and good.

Soltis: That, of course, is the other alternative. Actions are not right because God commands them. Instead, God commands them because they are right. But while this has the advantage of not making God seem arbitrary in His dealings with people, it also suggests that the difference between what is right and wrong is not dependent on God's will. If God commands that which is right because it is right, then there must be something that makes it right independently of God's willing it. In this way God doesn't seem very different from a wise and just human ruler. He commands what is just because it is just. However, the standard of rightness or justice must be independent of the fact that it is commanded. If that's so, we should be able to say what makes something right or wrong without having to decide if God has willed it.

Philosopher: Yes, yes. But you know it's more complicated than that. For example some theologians have held that God's commands express His nature, not His will. Plato's argument (or your version of it) doesn't seem as successful against that view.

Strike: Actually, I've always thought that what made theological ethics interesting had little to do with all this stuff about God's commands. It seems to me that what is important is that theological ethics has some distinctive ethical concepts that are not often included in secular ethics. I think such concepts as reconciliation and redemption are quite important even apart from talk about God. One might argue that a major part of religious ethics is about restoring relationships.

Student 2: That might even have a place for caring?

Strike: I would think so.

Philosopher: Well, I'm sure that's very nice, but poor Aristotle and Dewey are still out in the cold. And you certainly didn't have much to say about caring, redemption, and reconciliation in your book. Aristotle has a great deal to say about the development of character that's worth listening to, and Dewey has much to say about the philosophy of education.

Strike: I've always been impressed by Aristotle's views on character formation.

Soltis: And I have high regard for Dewey's educational theories.

Student 2: Well, if Professor Strike is big on relationships and Aristotle, and Professor Soltis likes Dewey's views on education, why doesn't any of this come out in the book?

Strike: One reason is that we don't see ourselves as answering questions like "What is the nature of a good life?" or "What is the nature of a good education?" We think of ourselves as addressing questions about how people who might disagree deeply about these things can cooperate and settle disputes in public institutions.

Student 1: I'm confused. Why, for example, would this lead you to ignore God?

Strike: Suppose that you and an atheist had to work together on some common project, perhaps providing an education for your children, and that you had to agree on some basis for your cooperation. How would you feel if the atheist insisted that atheism had to be part of the basis for your cooperation?

Student 1: Obviously I wouldn't like that. I'd refuse to cooperate.

Philosopher: And would you insist instead that the atheist accept your theism as a basis for your cooperation?

Student 1: Well, that doesn't really seem fair, although I do think he'd be better off if he agreed with me. I suppose, however, that if he isn't allowed to insist on his atheism, to be consistent, I can't insist that he agree with my theism.

Strike: If you can't insist on your theism, and he can't insist on his atheism, how would you find a basis for cooperation?

Student 1: Well, I suppose we would have to agree to treat our religious differences as private matters to be pursued outside of schools.

Student 2: And I suppose that we would have to discover some ethical concepts that we can agree on even though we disagree about religious convictions.

Philosopher: You might consider that if you insist on thinking this way about your "ethics for public institutions" you will have to discover ethical principles that are neutral to a great deal more than religion.

They may have to be neutral to most fully articulated views about a good life, and they might even have to be neutral to conflicting conceptions of a good education. After all, a lot of people who may want to cooperate in public institutions will disagree about such matters too.

Strike: I think that's basically right. The "public ethic" for a pluralistic society has to be neutral to a lot of important things. Its view of a good life and a good education will be a bit thin. That doesn't mean that "thicker" views about the best ways to live and about a good education aren't important. What it means is that, in a free society, we can't impose them.

Student 2: So what kinds of ethical concepts can people agree on even though they disagree deeply about such important matters?

Soltis: They have mostly to do with what is just or fair. I suppose that the ethical principles we talk about in this book would be good examples. Ideas such as free speech, due process, privacy, or democratic decision making seem the kinds of things that people who disagree about much might agree on as ways to cooperate fairly. For example, I'd be surprised if there's any special reason why theists and atheists would have to disagree about due process.

Student 2: But how about character development or relationships such as caring? Professor Strike seems to think that these are important to a well-considered ethic, but you don't say much about them.

Soltis: I agree with Professor Strike that these are important topics. In fact, I think they are important for the ethics of teaching. Teachers should be people of good character, and they should care about their students. At the same time, character and a capacity to care seem to us to be things that develop over a lifetime, and they are not primarily cognitive. It's not easy for me to see how we can reform people's character or turn them into caring people in a short book. But we do think we can help them understand what free speech and due process are about and how to think about ethics rationally so they may reach public decisions that are discussable and defensible.

Student 2: But you sound as if this "public ethic" of fairness and justice you talk about and an ethic of relationships are perfectly compatible. Don't some people treat them as alternatives?

Strike: It's true that some writers sound as though these views are opposed. But I don't quite see it that way.

Philosopher: And how do you see it?

Strike: It seems to me that an ethic of caring or other ethics to which relationships are central try to describe what human relationships are ideally like. Relationships such as love, or caring, or friendship are very important to the quality of people's lives. Moreover, in some contexts it is important that these relationships should be the central concern. Where they are, there is little need to worry about justice or about working out rules that detail the basis of cooperation. In families where people love each other and care about each other, there's often little need for discussion of fairness or justice. In fact, when friends or family members spend a lot of time worrying about fairness, that can be a sign that the friendship or the caring relationship is at risk.

Student 2: So you see justice as important in places where caring cannot be taken for granted?

Strike: That's right. Maybe in an ideal world human relations would be governed by friendship, love, or caring. But the world isn't always perfect. Moreover, many who have written about caring or friendship have emphasized that these are relationships that we have with particular people. We can't be friends with everyone, and we can't care for everyone. We have to decide how we can relate responsibly to those for whom we do not care. Another way to put it is that friendship and caring express ways to relate that people have found to be good and worthwhile ways to connect with some people. Justice tells us how we must relate to people however we feel about them and regardless of whether we care for them. The "public ethic" sets minimum standards. It's a kind of moral safety net.

Philosopher: Well, all of this seems doubtful to me, but at least I begin to get a clearer picture of why you included what you included and omitted what you omitted from this book. But why all this stuff about consequentialist and nonconsequentialist ethics?

Soltis: We did this because these two broad groups of ethical theories have historically been major ways in which philosophers have sought to justify various aspects of justice. Certainly anyone who grasps these arguments will have made a good start at understanding how philosophers have thought about the kinds of moral concepts that govern social cooperation in liberal democratic societies that respect pluralism, although there is much more to be learned.

Philosopher: But I have noticed that Professor Soltis grows silent when Professor Strike waxes eloquent about neutrality between differing conceptions of a good life.

Soltis: Hmm. Yes, sometimes I think Ken gets carried away here. I wonder if a viable educational system might not require a "thicker" conception of a good life than he will allow. There are also a few other things he's said that I'd like to repair.

Strike: Indeed, fine fellow and profound thinker though he is, I'm not entirely certain that Jonas has fully seen the light on several topics. Even worse, I change my mind on some of them two or three times a year.

Philosopher: So even though you two agree on enough to write a book, if I really probed your views deeply I might find some fundamental disagreements down there?

Strike: Could be. But we think the most important lesson of this book is that even when people disagree, even deeply, about the justification of ethical concepts, it's still possible for them to agree on some basic rules for what it means to treat people fairly.

Soltis: Actually, while I think that's an important observation, I think that the most important lesson of this book is that dialogue and reflection are required if people are to make progress on some difficult and important questions. No doubt my colleague and coauthor also has much respect for dialogue and reflection.

Strike: No doubt.

Philosopher: But to all dialogue there must come an end. I suggest that we devote our remaining moments to deciding who should pick up the tab for lunch. I think that since Professor Strike invited us to this conversation, he should repress his natural predilections to frugality and pick up the check.

Professor Strike, feeling some pain at the suggestion and silently asking the forgiveness of his Scottish ancestors, but noting the relieved looks on the students' faces and recalling that Professor Soltis paid the last time, picks up the bill and walks toward the cash register thinking ambiguous thoughts about the necessity of fairness.

Chapter 6

Supplemental Case Studies

The cases we have considered thus far were designed to illustrate moral issues and to get you to think about basic ideas regarding the ethics of teaching. Real-world ethical situations, however, do not just illustrate and provide food for thought—they require decision and action. As a moral person operating in the complex real world, you will need to identify legitimate moral interests and rights of others. As an educator, this means not only those of your students, but also of professional colleagues and staff, parents, and others. This requires the ability to empathize, to put yourself in another's place. You will also need to chart a reasonable course of action based on moral concepts and consequences that do the most good or least harm or uphold important principles. Sometimes you will even be called upon to justify your decisions and actions.

Of course, not all the instances of moral decision making and action that you will face will be emergencies or life threatening or challenged by others. In our daily dealings with people, we are always in a state of potential ethical relationship with each other in simple as well as complex and difficult ways. Part of what we hope to accomplish with this book is to sensitize you to that ever-present moral potential in human situations and to dispose you to treat it responsibly whenever you recognize it. Sometimes this will mean no more than showing respect for persons, for their privacy, or for equity. Sometimes it will require deeper reflection, searching analysis, careful judgment, and tactful action. Sometimes it will help if you share your thoughts, feelings, and reasons with others as you seek reflective equilibrium and your own moral growth as a person and as a professional.

Obviously, we cannot present the real world to you in this chapter, but we can provide a number of unanalyzed cases that touch on a broad range of moral concepts and potential consequences for you to think about. This will give you some practice in ethical thinking and theorizing as well as provide you with an opportunity to try to use some of the things you learned in this book. Ideally, these cases should be discussed with others. We have tried to make them the "next best thing" to real-world situations that can and do occur in everyday teaching situations. Most have been drawn from the experiences of practicing teachers.

Remember as you deal with these cases that part of what we have argued with regard to ethical objectivity is that ethical decision making is not just following the rules or applying the right moral principle and sticking to it no matter what. Considering the context, using your moral intuition to search for relevant underlying moral feelings, concepts, and principles, testing them and considering the present state of your moral theory and the rights, interests, feelings, and reasons of others—all may be necessary to reach a justifiable decision about a moral course of action.

Discussing these cases with others will give you an opportunity to think out loud and to hear others do so while the group tries objectively and rationally to reach a provisionally valid agreement in ethics. We think you will be surprised at the agreements reached regarding moral intuitions and the willingness of people not only to hear and respect others' views but also to accept good reasons for changing their own. This should be done not to reach consensus for its own sake, but to reach the most *morally* acceptable decision under the circumstances. Of course, there will be some disagreements and unsettled cases. The world is not neat and simple. Objective and rational discussion in moral matters offers no guarantee of successful reflective equilibrium in every case, but it does offer more promise for moral growth and moral sensitivity than does a relativistic policy of "to each his own."

The following procedures and suggestions may be helpful to you as you prepare to discuss the cases and do your own analyses. They should not be looked on as a recipe for reaching moral decisions. There are no such recipes. You will, of course, need to use your moral intuitions, consider consequences, empathize, search for alternatives, be reasonable and sincere. But there is no special or magical order for doing these things that will guarantee success. Creative ethical thinking needs to be cultivated by doing it with the proper attitudes and persistence.

1. Read a case through once quickly and reach a "seat of the pants" teacher decision in the case. Ask yourself what moral concept(s) or principle(s) or consequence(s) would explain and justify your decision as the teacher.

2. Reread the case and try to put yourself in the position of other major actors in the case. Playing those roles, do you see any legitimate claims or rights or ethical principles that might be advanced by the other persons in the case that might give you good reasons to alter your decision?

3. Reconsider the case from the point of view of the teacher. What central or basic moral concept(s) is (are) operative? Can you construct a consequentialist and a nonconsequentialist argument? Which appears stronger? Why? Can they work together? Do thought experiments with examples.

4. Discuss the case with others. Test your position with them. Be open to their ideas and reasons but be true to what you honestly consider to be the most compellingly reasonable moral position, yours or theirs, as it develops. Can a reflective equilibrium consensus on moral theory or principle be reached? Remember, the point of considering these cases is not just the practical one of solving a problem, but also being *ethical* in its solution and continuing your own development as a moral person. If consensus is reached, is it an accident of the similarity of the people in the room or is there reason to believe others would agree? Can you think of a plausible objection? Can you imagine how a person quite different from you might respond? If no consensus develops, can you find the basic points at issue? Are they always bound to be in conflict? What different moral theories do they lead to?

There is no end to the questions you can ask and think about regarding these cases as you explore and, we hope, become more sensitive to the ethics of teaching. It will probably be impossible for you and your class to examine and discuss all the cases in this chapter in the fullness required by an objective and rational approach. To assist you in selecting cases of interest and to give you an overview of what each is about, we have provided a schematic summary in table 1 at the end of this section. In it we have identified the case by its title and the topic it treats, the pages it appears on, and the central moral concepts or principles at issue. We hope that the cases in this chapter will challenge your thinking and develop your ethical sensitivities as educators and as moral persons.

You may find that a case can be made more realistic by having others assume the roles of the various individuals described in the case. Of course, you may wish to write and share your own cases based on personal experience. These are often the most realistic.

TABLE 1.   Summary of Case Studies

Page	Title and Topic	Concepts at Issue
100	"Teacher Burnout" Discovering alcoholism and poor teaching	Loyalties, obligation to educate, whistle blowing, equity
103	"Whose Rights: Students' or Parents'?" Abortion	Life, parents' rights, students' welfare, privacy, maturity
105	"You Get What You Pay For" Cut in funds, teacher gives advance placement class in home	Students' welfare, obligation to fellow teachers and teacher organizations
106	"Pledge of Allegiance" Self-confessed rule breaker, marijuana	Confidentiality, privacy, responsibility for enforcing school rules
108	"Teacher or Friend?" Students invited to parties at teacher's home	Professional and personal domains
109	"Professional Conduct: Two Cases" a. Students seek teachers' appraisal of principal and school policies b. Teacher reconsiders a team-teaching agreement	Professional relations, surveillance, agreements, due process
112	"College or Workforce?" Student put in vocational track; parents want college prep	Parents' and students' rights, professional judgment and consequences
114	"Values Clarification" Personal-values course questioned by parents	Teacher autonomy, parents' rights, teaching values

If you do decide to try writing your own cases, the following suggestions may be helpful:

1. It is best, and easiest, if you write about those matters with which you are familiar, issues that you have encountered in your own professional experience. Personal experience, observation, and analysis make it possible to write a realistic and meaningful case.
2. Try to present a problem that is encountered in teaching, and, through the case, make reference to underlying ethical issues. The case must have an issue, and you the writer must have a purpose. The case's purpose, its pedagogical objective, provides the writer with direction and guidance during the telling of the story.
3. The problem must be difficult, an ambiguous situation that is in need of decision and justification. Questions should not be too leading, rigid, or exhaustive, but should allow the reader some spontaneity and freedom of interpretation. Sometimes it is useful to make reference to more general issues that are embedded in the case.
4. In the actual writing of the case, it is necessary to set the scene. The first paragraph ordinarily describes the situation within which the story develops, and successive paragraphs introduce characters, their actions and points of view. Often these points of view are incompatible, but it is important that you make it possible for the reader to empathize with each character. The problem is developed and presented through the course of events that are reported by the writer until the moment of conflict or decision. Be sure to develop competing justifications for the conflicting points of view. End with some relevant questions or alternative courses of action that the reader might consider.
5. Reread your case as if you were someone else looking at it for the first time. Are the issues and facts clear? Do you feel that you have accomplished your original pedagogical objective? Revise, if necessary.

TEACHER BURNOUT

Michael Baker was a recent appointee to the history faculty at Woodrow Wilson Senior High School. He had been a good student in college and had done well as a student teacher, but he had many doubts about his preparedness for his new job. He was not an experienced teacher, and the real life of the classroom had not been fully described in his teaching manual. Michael wished that there was someone to whom he could speak about the daily problems and tasks of a high-school teacher. He needed a mentor.

He found a mentor, and a friend, in Frank Thompson. Mr. Thompson had taught history at Woodrow Wilson for twelve years, and he was thought to be an excellent teacher. He was a favorite with the student body, his classes were lively, and his students' scores in statewide examinations compared favorably with history scores at other schools.

Frank Thompson was willing to share his experience as a teacher. After work, over beers, he would regale Michael with stories of life at the school. Before long, Michael came to know the idiosyncracies and humors of his fellow teachers and even a bit of gossip about the students. Frank's information and support helped Michael to feel more comfortable in his work. Michael did not care to drink as much as Frank, but the occasional hangover was not too great a price to pay for the pleasant company and the tips on teaching.

Sometimes Frank would overdo the afterwork tippling, and it showed in his eyes the next morning. Occasionally, Mike would cover one of Frank's classes in his free time, while Frank recuperated over coffee in the faculty lounge. He did not mind doing a favor for a friend, and he thought that some exposure to Frank's classes would be a good experience for him. These students usually tested among the best in the history exam, and Michael wanted to find out why. Frank told him that he rarely used a planned lecture and that it would be good for Michael to take the plunge and trust his instincts in the classroom. The students worked hard, and they deserved a little fresh air.

Michael discovered that trusting his instincts was no guarantee of success. He probed the class with several questions on recent American history in order to get some idea of the state of their knowledge. However, most of the class did not respond, and those few answers he elicited were often wrong or irrelevant. Finally, out of exasperation, he asked the class what they ordinarily did with Mr. Thompson. He was told that the class usually spent most of the time talking about current events, television, and sports. In that case, asked Mr. Baker, how were they going to prepare for tests and the statewide examination? The students told him that Mr. Thompson always gave them a list of questions to study in preparation for tests. These questions, or some variations, were usually on the tests, and the students who prepared scored well. Mr. Thompson had promised that he would do the same for the statewide examination and, in fact, had already started preparing them in the same manner.

Michael was very disturbed by what he had been told in that class.

The students did not seem to learn very much history. Rather, they had been shepherded through a series of tests in such a way that they would grade well. Now, they were being coached for the state examinations. This did not seem right, and Michael decided to ask Frank Thompson about the situation.

Frank had recuperated, but he was still irritable. He was very blunt in his response. Mike's problem, he said, simply did not matter. Frank had learned a while ago that his work did not make that much difference in the lives of his students, and it was not making him very happy either. If Bozo the Clown were in front of the classroom, the results would be the same. The bright kids would do well, the dummies would fare poorly, and his efforts would not change the outcome very much. So, he had decided, why not make the whole process as painless as possible? Frank tried to make his time in the classroom pleasant, and he hoped that it would not interfere with his evenings. He provided his students interesting conversation and cursory instruction in the subject. If they were able to answer the series of questions that they had been given before the tests, he was satisfied, the students were satisfied, and no one was wiser. In the case of the state examination, he had a file of old exams that he used to prime the students for good performances. If necessary, with a few phone calls to various sources, he could find out what the trends were in the current test. If the students scored well with his help, he would be satisfied that he had done his job well, for grades were the bottom line that made him and the school look good. This is what he did, and he would continue to follow this procedure until that wonderful day when he qualified for a pension and could leave teaching. He told Mike Baker that it was none of his business.

Michael felt that it was his business, but he did not know what to do about his friend. Frank was in bad shape. He drank too much, neglected his duties, and the students were not being served adequately. Michael felt that he should tell someone.

Some Questions

1. Friendships and professional relationships are based on mutual trust, loyalty, and, among other things, respect. In this case, Michael has had his belief in these principles stretched to the breaking point. Do you think he has good reason to ''blow the whistle'' on Frank, to tell appropriate superiors about what is going on?
2. Has Frank done anything wrong? He does not drink in school or arrive drunk. He teaches to the test, but many teachers do that.

Moreover, state standardized tests are given to ensure equity of evaluation across different schools and districts. One could argue that Frank is doing the right thing. Are Frank's students being educated?
3. How might the principles of benefit maximization and respect for persons apply in this case?

WHOSE RIGHTS: STUDENTS' OR PARENTS'?

Lydia Simpson taught physical education and health education at a suburban high school. She had graduated from college a few years before and, while at school, had been active in intercollegiate athletics and various feminist groups. Lydia was young enough to remember clearly the confusion of adolescence, yet mature and able to speak of those decisions that mark our growth as adults. As a teacher, she attempted to imbue her students with a sense of self-worth and a knowledge of the opportunities that could be theirs as women in the modern world. As an adviser, she lent a sympathetic ear to her students' problems and aspirations. The girls saw her as a person worthy of emulation, and they responded to her concern in kind. Those bonds of mutual respect and affection, which can be among the greatest joys for a teacher, grew between Lydia and many of her students, extending beyond the confines of the school.

As a health educator and feminist, Lydia was determined that her charges become aware of their reproductive rights and responsibilities, for she knew that they would face difficult and complicated decisions about sexual behavior. In Lydia's classes, sex education was a matter of values clarification, as well as biology and human anatomy. In addition to detailed instruction in the facts of sexual life, the students discussed a variety of adult sexual practices and a number of related ethical views about these activities. Lydia emphasized that young men and women have several options they can pursue: celibacy, different forms of birth control, and, in unfortunate cases, abortion. Lydia attempted to make it clear to her students that, because their bodies and their futures were at issue, they had the right to make these decisions. In order that she not infringe upon their rights or stray from her obligations as a teacher, Lydia was careful that she offer a balanced presentation and not seem to espouse any one view. She hoped that her instruction and advice would be of some benefit and that all would work out well for her students in this sensitive area of life.

Things do not always work out well. A junior girl named Karen, one of Lydia's favorites, came to her one day in a very distressed state. Karen was pregnant, or at least thought that she was pregnant, for she was afraid to speak to her family doctor. She was also afraid to speak to her parents, who were quite religious and had tried to be strict with her. For this reason, she had been slow to approach them on the subject of birth control, and the results of her unguided experimentation had been unfortunate. She needed Lydia's help. Would she, Karen asked, take her to a clinic and, if necessary, advise her about an abortion?

Lydia was stunned, and she was confused about the proper course of action to follow. Several contradictory principles and emotions seemed to collide in the girl's question. As an independent-minded person and a feminist, Lydia felt that any woman as young as Karen could not sacrifice her present and future happiness because of one mistake. Abortion seemed to be the most likely alternative. However, as an educator, Lydia might not have the right to interject her opinion and active support into this sensitive situation. Some people, particularly Karen's parents, would consider this being party to a murder. Lydia realized that while Karen might have some rights concerning her future and reproductive freedom, her parents also had rights and an obligation to nurture and provide moral guidance for their daughter. Did Karen's right to privacy and freedom of action outweigh considerations of parental authority and parental right to know about the behavior of a minor? Lydia wished that there were one course of action or advice she could recommend that would balance these competing imperatives and still resolve the dilemma.

Some Questions

1. Respect for persons is a very fundamental ethical principle. Often, in debates over abortion, a pro or con position is based on claims about when or whether a fetus is a person. In this case, Karen and her parents are also candidates for respect as persons. Can you construct an argument for Karen's rights and for her parents' rights? Which would take precedence in this case? Why?
2. Lydia must weigh a number of obligations and potential consequences before she reaches a decision about taking Karen to a clinic. List as many of these as possible. In this case, which of these weighs most heavily and why? What would you decide to do if you were Lydia?

YOU GET WHAT YOU PAY FOR

In 1980, following in the footsteps of their forebears who organized the Boston Tea Party, the residents of Massachusetts once again rose up in protest against what they perceived to be burdensome taxation. Rather than dumping anything into Boston harbor this time, however, the citizens voted for a measure called Proposition 2½, which put limits on the ability of cities and towns in the state to assess property taxes. The subsequent loss in revenue forced the curtailment of municipal services of all kinds—police and fire departments were reduced, refuse collection was eliminated. Particularly hard hit were the public-school systems, where enrichment and other special programs, extracurricular activities, and sports were severely reduced or eliminated entirely.

Marshbury High School, a suburban school with a student body of approximately 1,200, had always enjoyed a reputation as one of the best public high schools in the state. Each year a large percentage of the graduating class had gone on to college, many of the students attending Ivy League and similarly selective schools. With the advent of Proposition 2½ and its consequences, however, the school had to lay off teachers and eliminate programs. Advanced Placement and enrichment programs as well as special education and sports had all gotten the axe. Those teachers in the system who were lucky enough to retain their jobs had responded to the treatment of their colleagues with a "rulebook slowdown." The taxpayers would get what they paid for and not a bit more.

Jerrold Ross, head of the history department, had been a popular and well-respected teacher in the system for nearly twenty years. He had always taken an exceptional interest in his students, especially the bright ones, and many of them had stayed in touch with him through college and beyond. Of all the bright students he had had over the years, however, the juniors in the AP history class this year were the best. He had taught them when they were sophomores and he had been looking forward to having them again as seniors. But because Proposition 2½ had forced the elimination of the AP program for the next year, these students would be part of his standard American history class with an enrollment of over 40.

Mr. Ross is not happy with this situation. He thinks the taxpayers were stupid to have voted the measure and shares his colleagues' disdain for them. But he does not feel, as they apparently do, that the children should suffer for the sins of their parents. Mr. Ross has decided to teach the AP curriculum to the kids who would have been in the class on his own time, in his own home. The students are enthusiastic, but the other teachers are not. They feel that Mr. Ross's decision shows callous disregard for the teachers who have lost their jobs and they are pressuring him to call off his plans for the independent effort. As a result, Mr. Ross has had a moment or two of doubt. Is he playing right into the hands of the shortsighted taxpayers? To whom does he owe the greatest allegiance—his students or his colleagues?

Some Questions

1. Mr. Ross is caught between his obligations to his students and to his fellow teachers. Arguments based on respect for persons and benefit maximization could be constructed to support either side. Are there other factors in this case that might give more weight to one group, students or fellow teachers, than the other?
2. Role-play a meeting at which Mr. Ross, one of his AP students, a laid-off teacher, a citizen who supports Proposition 2½, a parent of an AP and a non-AP student, and a teachers' union representative testify before the school board. What principles are at issue? Should the school board allow Mr. Ross to teach in his home? Do they have a right to tell Mr. Ross what he can do on his own time? Does the teachers' union have any claim on limiting Mr. Ross's end run on their "rulebook slowdown" stance?
3. Is this a case of democracy at work? What does that mean in a public-school setting? Where does authority reside? How can changes be brought about democratically?

PLEDGE OF ALLEGIANCE

Morningside Academy, a coeducational day school for 500 students in grades 7 through 12, was founded in 1904, in part for the purpose of helping "students to make their own decisions, assume responsibility for their choices, and respond sensitively to the needs of others." In recent years, under the stewardship of Headmaster Robert Jennings, the school has embodied a staunchly conservative philosophy of education.

One area of student life that reflects this philosophy concerns the use of drugs and alcohol by students. As headmaster, Mr. Jennings has taken an unequivocal stand against the use of these substances and has clearly articulated this position to both faculty and student constituencies. It is understood that a violation of this major school rule will result in immediate expulsion from the academy. Recently, for example, several popular seniors were expelled from Morningside when, a week before graduation, a night watchman discovered them drinking from a small flask in the locker room after the Spring Sports Banquet. In small-group meetings with advisers the next day, students were reminded of the academy's policy.

The adviser system is thought by students, parents, and school administration to enhance the goals of the academy through friendly and supportive interaction and dialogue. Ginny, an eighth-grade student, has scheduled an appointment for the third time this week with her adviser, Mr. Stimson, having broken two previous appointments. During the meeting, she seems on edge and unfocused, though clearly anxious to talk about something. Toward the close of their disjointed conference, Ginny ultimately confesses that on two occasions in recent weeks she and another student have slipped behind the academic building to try marijuana. Upon further questioning, Ginny admits that it was "fun," but that she is afraid she might do it again. Apparently she is worried about being caught and having to suffer the consequences, which, she clearly understands, include expulsion from Morningside. Will Mr. Stimson please help her, Ginny implores, as she, late for her next class, rushes out of his office. Aside from chewing gum in study hall, a minor infraction of the rules, Ginny is on High Honor Roll with an $A-$ average. Ginny is Headmaster Jennings's youngest daughter.

Mr. Stimson, in his second year of teaching and coaching at Morningside Academy, finds himself in a quandary, puzzled by how to respond to his advisee's confession. Should he go to the school's administration with this information, Mr. Stimson will have broken the bond of trust that allowed Ginny to discuss her situation in confidence in the first place. And if the school authorities become involved, Ginny most likely will be expelled from Morningside Academy for her confessed misbehavior.

And yet, Mr. Stimson's two-year probationary period is over at the end of this school year and he faces an administrative evaluation for the renewal of his contract. Should Ginny be caught smoking marijuana on campus, he worries, and school officers discover that he had prior knowledge of Ginny's activities without bringing them to their attention, his professional conduct would be in serious question and his contract in jeopardy. That Ginny is Headmaster Jennings's daughter only compounds the dilemma.

Some Questions

1. This is a case of mixed obligations. One is to a student who has assumed a confidential relationship and the other is to being responsible for following school rules. Which should take precedence here? Why?
2. There is also an important dimension of self-interest and prudence in this case. Clearly it is not wrong to consider one's own well-being in addition to the well-being of others. If you were Mr. Stimson, how might you try to protect yourself in this situation? Could you do this ethically? On what grounds would you defend your action?

TEACHER OR FRIEND?

Block City is a small factory town in upstate New York that is noted for its tool-and-die industry. The families who live in Block City are second- and third-generation Americans who take pride in their accomplishments and the sort of life they have carved out in the town. A significant source of civic pride is Block City High School, which has established a reputation for having one of the best scholastic football teams in the country. The students who play on the varsity football team enjoy the popularity and prominence that accompanies the team's achievements. They hold a special position in the social life of the town, because both their peers and adult fans, of which there are many, hold them in great esteem.

Ron Nelson, the coach of the football team, is a young, good-looking twenty-seven-year-old who was hired the year he graduated from college. Mr. Nelson is an alumnus of Block City, and he was an all-star halfback on the varsity football team throughout his high school career. During his tenure as coach he has upheld the winning tradition at the school. Mr. Nelson is a very enthusiastic coach, and he has good rapport with many of the students. They often seek his advice on a variety of problems that range from grades to girlfriends. Mr. Nelson also helps junior and senior football players select colleges and athletic programs, and many Block City footballers have received scholarships to well-known universities.

During the past year, a select group of football players, known as the "inner circle," has become very close to Mr. Nelson. They often spend Saturdays and some weeknights at his home, watching football games on television or simply hanging around socializing. To be invited to Coach Nelson's gatherings gives a student a certain extra bit of status at the school.

There has been some talk in the administration and among some of the faculty about the propriety of Mr. Nelson's relationship with these students. Rumors have indicated that beer drinking and raucous parties take place at his house when the students are there. Nobody has approached Mr. Nelson, and he ignores the rumors.

Mr. Nelson has planned another party for a weekend in early December in order to mark the conclusion of another successful football season. It will be a reunion for some of his old football buddies, many of whom now recruit or coach for university teams. He has invited the better players on the team, and they cannot wait to go. It will be fun, and they will be able to meet some people who will be able to further their football careers.

Word of this party has caused some dispute at the school. Some faculty members have approached the principal, saying that it was unprofessional of Mr. Nelson to invite these students to a party of this sort. Alcoholic beverages would be served, and the players were not old enough to drink. It is not unlikely that the party will get out of hand. These faculty members have demanded that the principal reprimand Mr. Nelson and have him withdraw his invitation to the students. Others feel that the idea for a party is harmless and may allow some of the players to make some helpful contacts. Besides, it is not anyone's business what the coach and his players do outside of school.

Some Questions

1. Where does the private behavior of teachers start and the professional domain for which they are publicly accountable end?
2. If Mr. Nelson had been working on the side as a talent scout for the state university's football coach, would this significantly alter the case? Why or why not?
3. Can you think of things we ordinarily take to be private or personal matters that a teacher might be held accountable for to a school principal or school board? What would be the grounds for making such claims?

PROFESSIONAL CONDUCT: TWO CASES

Janet Wyler had taught history for several years at a junior college. Tired of lecturing and longing for a change, she decided to try working at a different level in the educational system. The public schools were not hiring, so she accepted a job with a small, conservative, church-affiliated school at a considerable reduction in salary, even though she was neither conservative nor religious. She agreed to teach four sections of freshman history and one of remedial junior English, a total of 143 students.

Janet found teaching high school to be challenging and exciting. She liked being with the students and even relished lunchroom duty, for it afforded her the opportunity to observe student interaction. Accustomed to dealing with adults and high-school graduates, she treated her students with respect and genuine care. In a short time she developed an easy relationship with her classes and became known as an adult who could be approached. Janet made a habit of coming to work early every day in order to be available for those students who wanted to shoot the breeze or needed to talk seriously. There was usually someone waiting for her, occasionally a student other than her own or even a fellow teacher.

Much as she loved and was rewarded by her work, she found dealing with the school's administration to be very difficult. Janet's philosophy of education emphasized discovery, opening the world for the student. She attempted to create a proper relaxed atmosphere for this. The school's position stressed adherence to rules and strict norms of acceptable behavior. She had a difficult relationship with the principal and the attendance secretary, both of whom, she felt, should never have been allowed near children. Janet had observed that neither person seemed to like or trust people, and they were unpleasantly manipulative in their handling of others. Both had indicated to Janet that they found her relationships with students to be unprofessional because she did not maintain a proper distance.

Janet believed that the administration's views adversely affected the rest of the faculty and the student body, as well as herself. No one was given any freedom or responsibility at all.

Each classroom had a two-way speaker, and it was known that the principal and the attendance secretary occasionally listened to class sessions. On the third day of school, Janet had been called on the carpet for allowing excessive noise in her classroom. When she apologized to her neighbors, she discovered that the complaint had not come from them but from the attendance secretary, who had been eavesdropping on the public-address system.

During faculty meetings, Janet had pointed out the need for a student lounge and had suggested the creation of a mutual-help program in which students could tutor each other. She was told that students could not be left to themselves and could not be trusted.

Janet faced a year at a school where she was often in direct opposition to administrative goals and philosophy. It was a time of great stress, during which she had to make and defend many difficult decisions. Two cases will illustrate Janet's dilemma.

Case One

Janet's relationship with her remedial English class is a very special one indeed. They have been put in a remedial group because not one of them cares a whit for school. From the very first day Janet has made it her most important priority to help them build self-confidence and develop a positive attitude toward their work. She believes that they will learn only when they want to learn and that that can happen only when they feel good about themselves. As a result of the atmosphere that Janet creates, discussions are frank and challenging. Reading books like *The Bell Jar, Flowers for Algernon,* and *The Pigman* provides ample fuel for discussion, and the class spends a good part of the year reading and writing poetry. Janet is pleased and proud to note improvement in both depth of thought and the level of articulation among the students.

Several weeks after Christmas vacation, a discussion arises in class about rules and their necessity. Before Janet is able to react, the discussion moves toward an intense protest against school policy, including personal criticism of the principal and the attendance secretary. The discussion becomes vociferous and emotional, the students venting three years of frustration and anger. Feelings become so intense that Janet can only sit back and let the storm pass. Then she is faced with a series of very difficult questions, the first of which is posed by one of her students: "Ms. Wyler," the student asks, looking at Janet with obvious trust and respect, "what's your opinion?"

Some Questions

1. Often teachers find themselves not in total agreement with a school policy or not very impressed with the leadership skills of a principal. Would it be wrong to share these opinions with students? If you were Janet, what would you say to the students in this case, and how would you justify your decision?
2. Is this a case of surveillance or supervison? Could you construct arguments for and against the policy of monitoring classes by two-way speakers? Which argument carries the most weight? Why?

Case Two

Janet teaches history across the hall from the freshman English class, which is taught by Mr. Burry. John Burry, known affectionately as

Burry, or Furry Burry when he is sporting his winter beard, is an explosive, charming, funny, and very popular teacher. The boys think he is terrific, and many girls have a crush on him. This is so despite the fact that he is considered one of the toughest teachers at the school. Freshmen are known to dread Burry's tests two weeks in advance, and he has one of the highest proportions of failing grades in the school. He and Janet share a deep affection for the children, a lunch period, and off-beat senses of humor. Janet has observed him teach and has learned from him. She likes and respects him. They plan to experiment during the last month of school and teach as a team, synthesizing the two disciplines and mixing their classes.

It is a shock to Janet when she hears several uncomplimentary things about Mr. Burry. She is approached by the entire honors section of the history class and is told a tale indicating that he is guilty of insensitivity, unfairness, temper tantrums, and racial prejudice. Janet finds the accusations hard to believe, but the students are adamant, and one is near tears. They claim that Burry threw a book at a student. They *saw* it. Another student says that Mr. Burry called him a "Chink." The class is agitated and upset. Janet realizes that their emotions are real and that they feel persecuted by Burry. She finds this hard to believe, but she must deal with this. She respects Mr. Burry as a teacher and likes him very much as a person. She is already committed to work with him. Obviously his class is not being monitored by the administration. What can she do?

Some Questions

1. Does Janet have a right to renege on her agreement to team teach with Mr. Burry? What would be just cause for doing so in this case?
2. Are there issues of due process in this case? Even if true, does the evidence students present make a case for the presence of racial prejudice in Mr. Burry's class?

COLLEGE OR WORKFORCE?

Central High School is the sole secondary school for Iron City, an aging northeastern industrial town. Iron City has seen better days and suffers from many of the problems that afflict our older towns, but Central High School has continued to serve the townspeople in the face of changing economics, demographics, and vocational aspirations.

Two facts about Iron City's population are important for any analysis of the school's place in the life of the town. Some residents of Iron City, Irish and Polish workers who have been in the mills and shops for generations, have great hopes for their children. They want them to make a better life by attending college and escaping the life of the mills. In recent years, their wishes on the subject have been reflected in an increased commitment to academic counseling and college preparatory courses at Central High School.

Another group has also had great impact on the town and the school. During the last twenty years large numbers of Latin Americans have arrived in Iron City, and their presence has affected the cultural life of the town and the educational mission of the schools. Central High School has sought to ease the process of assimilation for this group by emphasizing language instruction and instituting courses in cultural history. Yet, in the great melting pot, some things do remain the same. These Hispanic students now hold places in vocational education classes that formerly had been filled by first-generation Irish and Polish youngsters.

Norman Anderson, the principal of Central High School, has been satisfied with this state of affairs. He feels that the school provides an adequate, sometimes excellent, education for its students and serves the town in a suitable manner. The curriculum is balanced in such a way that it allows each student to pursue individual needs and interests, and the guidance department takes an active role in the process of selection. The rising numbers of graduates who attend college has been a source of pride for Mr. Anderson.

Given these perceptions, it is not surprising that Mr. Anderson has had some difficulty understanding the complaints of Mrs. Virginia Cruz, the mother of a sophomore student at the school. According to Mrs. Cruz, her son, Dennis, has been treated unfairly by his guidance counselor. Dennis Cruz intends to continue his education after high school and wishes to register for college preparatory courses. However, his adviser, Mrs. Kennedy, does not think that he will do well in these courses and has recommended that he register for the vocational education program instead. In Mrs. Cruz's opinion, the adviser has no right to turn Dennis away from his dreams at such an early age, when many other students are given a fair chance. In fact, she feels that this is an example of Mrs. Kennedy's prejudice. Mrs. Cruz has observed that a disproportionate number of Hispanic students are enrolled in vocational education courses at Central High School, and more often than not, they are advised to apply for apprenticeships or join the armed forces upon graduation, rather than apply for college admission. Mrs. Cruz believes that these practices should cease, for they are implicitly racist and discouraging to her son. He should receive the same sort of education and encouragement as other students. She will pursue this matter in a more assertive manner unless her son's wishes are acknowledged.

Mr. Anderson requested a conference with Mrs. Catherine Kennedy, the head of the guidance department, in order to discuss this question. She has informed him that her decision is not a matter of prejudice at all. Rather, her recommendations are the result of a realistic and objective evaluation of the student's chances for academic and vocational success. Dennis Cruz has not been a top student, and his grades and test scores support this conclusion. Like many Hispanic students, he does not possess the language skills and cultural background that would enable him to do well in college. In Mrs. Kennedy's opinion, she would be remiss in her responsibility as an educator to say or do otherwise. Furthermore, the financial burdens of higher education would be too great for the parents to bear. It would be unfair to recommend any other course of action and leave Dennis Cruz unprepared for those situations that he will have to face in the workaday world. Besides, the existing system has been the path to success for other immigrant groups, and it is probably the best policy to pursue at this time.

Some Questions

1. In this case, both perceptions and concepts of fairness are in conflict. It is obvious that the school official and the parent perceive the present situation differently. Is this an example of prejudice or a realistic view of the way things work in a heterogeneous society?
2. Should the application of this principle of equality of opportunity be extended to include open access to training and higher education for all? How might Mrs. Cruz and Mrs. Kennedy argue their respective positions with each other?
3. Should the school serve as society's sorting mechanism?

VALUES CLARIFICATION

Tom Henderson teaches at Central High School in Kenton, a small exurban community about thirty-five miles from a major metropolitan center. Long unaffected by the tempo and changes of modern life, Kenton is now in the midst of transition from a sleepy rural town to a sophisticated satellite city of the emerging high-tech economy. The landscape presents an incongruous blend of farms and research laboratories, and residents work at occupations that range from dairy farming to computer programming.

After reading a series of books on the subject, Tom decided to develop and teach a unit in values clarification. It went over very well with the students, and each time he presented it he found that the students became more receptive to the subject and their discussions became increasingly earnest and wide ranging. Eventually, Tom designed and offered an entire course called "Decision Making," which he hoped would help the youngsters to sort out their own beliefs and autonomous lifestyles. The course involved role playing, sensitivity encounters, questionnaires, and other strategies taken from the literature on the subject. The curriculum committee of the local board of education approved the course.

The central idea of the "Decision Making" course is that a person creates his/her own values through decisions. We must choose our own values by our words and actions, free, as much as is possible, from authority, conditioning, and social pressures. Only in this way do values become authentically our own. There is no way to prejudge situations, and no other person can really tell us what is right or wrong. Tom uses realistic exercises concerning such subjects as lifeboat ethics and food shortages to press home his point. He is not so much concerned that his students come up with pat answers as he is that they immerse themselves in problematic situations that test and stretch their beliefs.

Some of the parents were surprised by the new topics of dinner table conversation that their children brought home from school, and some became annoyed at the orientation of the course. In their opinion these exercises served to confuse and destroy values, not clarify them. They claimed that the course was the exact opposite of what wholesome moral guidance should be. For example, one parent complained that her daughter had told her that stealing could be justified under certain circumstances. So, she said, if her child "chose freely" to steal because she thought that it was justified by the situation, who would sit with her in juvenile court, the school? In the end, who is to be responsible for the values children learn while growing up, and whose desires are to determine school policy on these matters?

Another criticism was that the endless sequence of games and questionnaires tended to place the trivial and the profound on the same level. For example, one survey asked these sorts of questions:

Do you enjoy watching television?
Do you enjoy attending church or synagogue?
Do you prefer the country or the city?
Do you like baseball?

It was as if baseball and religion were assumed to hold the same degree of importance in a person's life; possibly not, if one preferred one over the other. It did not seem to make much difference in this approach. How were the parents to inculcate cherished values and emphasize the importance of a hierarchy of beliefs in life, if these beliefs were treated as subjects for surveys and role playing that were all on the same level? Kenton used to be an orderly town in which people knew what was right and how to act, but the rush into modern times was washing all that away. What was so bad about the old-fashioned morality that it needed to be clarified?

After much complaining and parental pressure, the director of guidance, Tom Henderson, and several other teachers who advocated the new approach met with the parents in a stormy PTA session. Their primary defense was that they saw themselves not as inculcating new values or destroying the old morality but as engaging in an effort to teach students to think for themselves and to identify clearly the values that their parents, churches, and society have already established as important. Nevertheless, the parents continued to oppose the course, saying that the family, not the school, was the proper forum for exploring morality and that the course should be dropped from the curriculum.

This case presents a quandary for those who are interested in the relation of ethics, moral education, and the school. Many people complain that the schools have become amoral or immoral and that they should become more concerned with inculcating values. However, when this is attempted it is often said that the schools espouse the wrong morality or that they should not be involved in this activity at all.

Some Questions

1. Should schools be engaged in moral education?
2. Is moral education the teaching of a code of ethics, values clarification, teaching how to reason objectively about ethical decision making, or creating a caring and just environment? Some, all, or other than these? What are the differences between them?
3. How would you approach the teaching of ethics in your classes?

Annotated Bibliography

Aristotle. *Nicomachian Ethics,* trans. W. D. Ross. New York: Oxford University Press, 1980.

An important classical text on the nature of the virtues.

Baier, Kurt. *The Moral Point of View.* New York: Random House, 1965.

Treats individual and social rules of reason and how they affect moral judgment.

Bayles, Michael D., and Henley, Kenneth. *Right Conduct: Theories and Applications.* New York: Random House, 1989.

A good selection of basic readings on natural law, rights, contractarianism, and utilitarianism followed by applications to problem cases of abortion, euthanasia, the death penalty, pornography, AIDS, business ethics, future generations, and war.

Beck, Robert N., and Orr, John B. *Ethical Choice: A Case Study Approach.* New York: Free Press, 1970.

The writings of classical and modern ethicists are excerpted and applied to contemporary problems.

Bellah, Robert; Madsen, Richard; Sullivan, William; Swidler, Ann; and Tipton, Steven. *Habits of the Heart.* New York: Harper & Row, 1985.

An attack on individualism and an affirmation of the importance of community in American life.

Bok, Sissela. *Lying: Moral Choice in Public and Private Life.* New York: Vintage, 1979.

Addresses the possible justifications and consequences of withholding the truth.

Bok, Sissela. *Secrets.* New York: Pantheon, 1982.

Discusses the right and obligation to keep secrets and those situations in which keeping secrets may not be justified.

Brennan, Joseph Gerard. *Ethics and Morals.* New York: Harper & Row, 1973.

A very readable treatment of classical and contemporary ethical theories and a consideration of such topics as morality and sex, love, death, and war and the state.

Bricker, David. *Classroom as Civic Education*. New York: Teachers College Press, 1989.

Bricker argues that cooperative learning and more emphasis on community are essential to the achievement of the goals of a liberal society.

Callan, Eamonn. *Autonomy and Schooling*. Montreal, Quebec: McGill-Queen's University Press, 1988.

A discussion of the concept of autonomy in the context of an argument for a child-centered education.

Dewey, John. *Reconstruction in Philosophy*. Boston: Beacon Press, 1957.

A good description of Dewey's views on science and philosophy, together with his views on the application of the scientific method to ethical problems.

Dworkin, Ronald. *Taking Rights Seriously*. Cambridge, Mass.: Harvard University Press, 1977.

A discussion of legal and ethical philosophy with a good chapter on affirmative action.

Frankena, William. *Ethics*. Englewood Cliffs, N.J.: Prentice-Hall, 1973.

A good introductory work on ethics.

Gilligan, Carol. *In a Different Voice*. Cambridge, Mass.: Harvard University Press, 1982.

This book argues that popular views of moral education exclude the female voice in that they ignore the importance of caring and relationships in ethics.

Girvetz, Harry K. *Beyond Right and Wrong*. New York: Free Press, 1973.

A thorough treatment of ethical skepticism and an argument for "objective relativism" in ethics.

Goodlad, John; Soder, Roger; and Sirotnik, Kenneth. *The Moral Dimensions of Teaching*. San Francisco: Jossey-Bass, 1990.

A collection of essays emphasizing the importance of the moral in an adequate conception of teaching.

Gutmann, Amy. *Democratic Education*. Princeton, N.J.: Princeton University Press, 1987.

A discussion of ethics and educational policy emphasizing the central role of democracy in educational thought.

Habermas, Jürgen. *Moral Consciousness and Communicative Action*. Cambridge, Mass.: MIT Press, 1990.

A defense of "discourse ethics" that treats dialogue as central to ethical decision making.

Hare, R. M. *Applications of Moral Philosophy*. Berkeley: University of California Press, 1972.

A lucid treatment of many moral concerns, including such things as relativism, the moral development of adolescents, the morality of governmental acts, and peace; deals with such questions as "What is life?" and "Can I be blamed for following orders?"

Hume, David. *An Inquiry Concerning Human Understanding*. New York: Liberal Arts Press, 1957.

A classic and comprehensive statement by the quintessential empiricist on matters of epistemology, human nature, and ethics.

Kant, Immanuel. *Critique of Practical Reason*, trans. Lewis W. Beck. Indianapolis, Ind.: Bobbs-Merrill, 1956.

The classical statement and defense of a nonconsequentialist ethical position. Hard reading, but worthwhile.

Levine, Alan H., and Cary, Eve. *The Rights of Students*. New York: Discus, 1977.

An American Civil Liberties Union handbook on constitutional rights.

MacIntyre, Alisdair. *After Virtue*. South Bend, Ind.: University of Notre Dame Press, 1982.

A recent influential critique of modern ethical theories and a defense of an Aristotelian viewpoint.

Mill, John Stuart. *On Liberty*. Indianapolis, Ind.: Bobbs-Merrill, 1956.

The classic arguments for freedom of opinion and lifestyle.

Mill, John Stuart. *Utilitarianism*. Reprinted in *The Utilitarian*. New York: Doubleday, 1961.

An excellent and brief statement of utilitarianism.

Niebuhr, Reinhold. *Moral Man and Immoral Society*. New York: Charles Scribner's Sons, 1932.

A classical discussion of ethics from a Christian perspective.

Noddings, Nel. *Caring: A Feminine Approach to Ethics and Moral Education*. Berkeley: University of California Press, 1984.

A discussion of caring and its implications for education.

Peters, R. S. *Ethics and Education*. London: George Allen & Unwin, 1970.

A discussion of several ethical concepts, such as punishment and equality, in an educational context.

Rawls, John. *A Theory of Justice*. Cambridge, Mass.: Harvard University Press, 1971.

Possibly the best contemporary statement of a liberal theory of social justice.

Rubin, David. *The Rights of Teachers*. New York: Discus, 1971.

An American Civil Liberties Union handbook on constitutional rights.

Shaver, James P., and Strong, William. *Facing Value Decisions*, 2nd ed. New York: Teachers College Press, 1982.

Explores values education within a democratic context and the rational foundations of values.

Strike, Kenneth. *Educational Policy and the Just Society*. Urbana, Ill.: University of Illinois Press, 1982.

A discussion of the concepts of liberty, equality, and rationality as applied to a range of educational problems.

Strike, Kenneth. *Liberty and Learning*. New York: St. Martin's Press, 1982.

Develops a theory of liberty for education. Contains chapters on academic freedom and students' rights.

Strike, Kenneth; Haller, Emil; and Soltis, Jonas. *The Ethics of School Administration*. New York: Teachers College Press, 1988.

A discussion of ethical issues in school administration. The book is modeled on *The Ethics of Teaching*.

Toulmin, Stephen. *Reason in Ethics*. Cambridge, U.K.: Cambridge University Press, 1970.

    Contrasts different ethical theories and points to a parallel between common sense and ethical reasoning.

Index